W9-BZY-938

SHAKESPEARE AND HIS PLAYERS

Martin Holmes

JOHN MURRAY

Printed in Great Britain
by W & J Mackay Limited, Chatham
0 7195 2583 7

To the Memory of
OTTO SALLMANN
1867–1967
who devoted so great a part
of his hundred years of life
to the enjoyment of Shakespeare
and the communication of that
enjoyment to others

Contents

Illustrations

PLATES

FIGURES IN TEXT

Figures 1, 2, 3, 4, 5, 11, 12, 13, 15 and 16 are reproduced from Vecellio's Costumes of the World, *1590*
Figures 6, 7, 10 and 14 are reproduced from Holinshed's Chronicles, *1577*
Figures 8 and 9 are reproduced from Evelyn's Numismata, *1697*

By Way of Prologue

Scholars, poets and antiquaries have written so much, and so well, about Shakespeare in the last three centuries that by sheer quality and quantity they may have done him an involuntary disservice. Matthew Arnold's famous sonnet beginning, 'Others abide our question. Thou art free,' carries with it a suggestion that any sort of questioning, let alone criticism, would be pointless and irreverent. Nearer our own day, A. C. Bradley has discussed the four great tragedies, and the nature of tragedy itself, with a deep and sensitive consideration of the text, but practically no attempt to equate it with the conditions of the theatre for which the plays were written. Both schools of thought have their followers still, some regarding the Sacred Swan as a divinity to be revered from afar (and therefore to have no connection with anyone so humdrum as the subject of the Droeshout portrait or the Stratford memorial bust), others laying him, as it were, under the lights of the operating-theatre to be anatomized for the instruction of students; and we can understand, and should respect, the views of both, without necessarily feeling obliged to share them. But there is yet another view to be considered, the view so honestly and explosively expressed to Fanny Burney by George III. 'Was there ever such *stuff* as great part of Shakespeare? Only one mustn't say so! But what think you?—what? Is there not sad stuff?—what?—what?' As early as 1785, it seems, people had got into the way of reading Shakespeare so dutifully, and staging him so peculiarly, that they had to a great extent forgotten how to enjoy him, and had transferred their admiration to his interpreters upon the stage. We still do the same. The best way to escape is to consider the poet's own day, when a play had to make its impression by its initial impact on the eye, the ear and, through them and only through them, on the heart and mind.

This belief must be the justification of the following chapters. Most of them are based on talks given at one time or another to various bodies, but the first was a paper written for the 1959 volume of *Essays and Studies*, edited that year by the late Dorothy Margaret Stuart—always to be remembered with gratitude and affection—and published by the English Association, to whom I am indebted for permission to reproduce it here.

I

The Elizabethan Approach

The London citizens who first enjoyed Shakespeare's plays did so in the theatre, and in the theatre alone. Over the space of 15 years, 14 plays were published more or less unofficially as individual quarto texts, some of them very bad ones, but it was not until 1623, when he had been seven years dead, that his collected plays (except for *Pericles, Prince of Tyre*) were available in one volume, the famous First Folio, with a preface advising the reader to 'Read him, therefore, and again, and again, and if then you do not like him, surely you are in some manifest danger not to understand him'. The advice is still good, but we may well be apt to forget that in its day it was not only good but revolutionary. No such work had been published before—a volume of 36 plays, some of them 30 years old, and all, or almost all, of them belonging to an outmoded fashion gently ridiculed by the up-and-coming dramatists of the reign of King James. Yet published it was, and published in the firm conviction that there would be a public for it. Playgoers might wish to revive memories of a piece that had stirred them in the theatre by reading it—and possibly re-reading in some places and skipping in others—in the contemplative quiet of the study, and to increase their knowledge and enjoyment of the author by finding what other plays he had written, that they themselves had not had the chance to see performed.

That, after all, is very much our attitude today. We base our knowledge of the plays upon our study of the printed texts rather than our impressions of their effect in performance, and there is a real danger that we may concentrate over-much on the subtleties, real or imagined, of the author's deeper meaning and find ourselves, in his first editors' phrase, in some manifest danger not to understand him. We have reasonable opportunities of seeing a certain number of the best-known plays, but not so much chance of seeing the whole 37, and it is natural that from our youth up we should think of Shakespeare's work as something to be read rather than watched or listened to. There is much enjoyment to be found that way, and unquestionably we gain much from the study of the lines and the slow, measured relish

Typical English young man and woman of the respectable citizen class, such as might attend a performance at the Theatre or the Curtain.

oi the poetry, and of the philosophy behind it. At the same time, there is something that we miss, and something that deserves better than to be ignored.

Briefly speaking, it is one simple thing—the author's intention. Shakespeare wrote his lines to be spoken in a theatre, to an audience that had come to be entertained, and he could not afford to dwell too long, or to let the audience dwell too long, on points that called for serious contemplation. The great soliloquies, for instance, are not only poetry, they are drama, the unfolding of the processes of a man's or woman's mind, and at the end of any one of them we are that much further on in our understanding of the speaker than we were at the beginning. Words, lines and phrases have to create an immediate impression at the moment of hearing, whether or not that impression lasts in the hearer's mind as the scene goes on. There is no time for going back and pondering, the word or phrase must have its immediate effect, since another is fast upon its heels and will not wait the hearer's leisure. Nowadays we can refresh our memories, or repeat our sensations, by studying the text upon the printed page, but Shakespeare's original audiences could not do anything of the sort, and he had no reason to suppose, when he wrote, that they would ever want to. He had to make his effects at first hearing, or not at all.

The more clearly we keep the thought of the theatre in our minds, the more variety and interest do we find as we read the plays. It is no longer Shakespeare who is speaking, but Hamlet or Rosalind or Falstaff, and they are all different. Let us forget for a moment that sublime figure of the Immortal Swan, who infused something of his own splendour into every character he created, and look instead at that pop-eyed, bald-headed little man whose genius could turn out kings, lovers, villains and ordinary vulgar persons who were all intensely and triumphantly themselves and owed nothing to each other nor even, noticeably, to the individual whose imagination had produced them all. It is this variety that is so important. In printed texts the words 'They fight' or 'Enter a Messenger' occur again and again, because there are not many other words in which one can say so, and we are not encouraged to differentiate one fight, or one messenger, from another. As soon as we see them in performance, however, we see how very different they can be, not only in their natures but in their relation to the story and their effect upon it. They have stopped being 'just Shakespeare' and are part of history or romance instead.

Looking at the plays in this way, as devised to interest,

entertain and satisfy a paying public, we find it possible to do more than imagine ourselves as members of an Elizabethan or Jacobean audience. With a very little knowledge of stage conditions, ancient or modern, and of the ordinary tastes of an ordinary playgoer, we can see the plays not only from the spectator's point of view but from the actor's into the bargain. It is all very well to read a long speech, or a brisk passage of dialogue, and admire the poetry, the tenderness or the wit, but it is still more illuminating to consider such a passage occasionally from the transmitting rather than the receiving end. The speech takes on a different quality at once. Instead of being a piece of Shakespeare to be respected, it becomes the expression of somebody's feelings—the character's, primarily, not the author's—and its object is to convey information, or to arouse an emotion of some sort, or possibly both at once. One finds oneself considering afresh what the words actually *mean*, what impression they are intended to convey, and how best one can convey that impression in the process of delivering them. In other words, the passage is coming to life.

Sometimes it fails to do so, and the reader turns from actor to producer. When Hamlet has quarrelled with Laertes at the edge of Ophelia's grave, he suddenly and very naturally tries to make amends, with the words:

> What is the reason that you use me thus?
> I loved you ever, but it is no matter.

What is one to make—what is Hamlet to make—of that second line? Is it all of a piece, and, as A. C. Bradley claimed for it in his *Shakespearean Tragedy*, an expression of the return of 'the old weary misery' in which nothing matters any more? Or is there a change of intention in the middle of the line—is Laertes dismissing the courtesy and brusquely turning away, so that Hamlet abandons his attempt with a word of apology? That is a point for the producer to decide, and the reader, in considering it, may find himself looking at the passage with a producer's eye, and ultimately making his own decision.

This is just as it should be. We have got to the stage of considering the practical problems of interpreting the plays as written, and the next step, if we care to take it, leads us to conjectures even more intriguing. We have looked into the meaning of the dialogue that Shakespeare has written, and the likeliest ways of making that dialogue effective on the stage, but now comes the fascinating, tantalizing question in each play—*why did he choose to do it like that?* How much of the form is accepted stage-custom, and how much his own individual variation? Where did he vary it, and is it possible to guess why?

Take, for instance, those little conversational scenes between two or three characters only, and minor characters at that, which are to be found throughout the plays and which are often omitted in performance, to the detriment of the play. They have a reason for being there, and on examination it is not too difficult to find. In a modern (but not a *too* modern) theatre there are moments when tension has been brought to its height, sustained for a while and then mercifully relaxed, whereupon the curtain comes down, the house-lights go up, and the audience can relax likewise. Shakespeare could not count on such variations of lighting or stage-picture, but he could count on variations of mood and verbal cadence, and he was masterly in the use of them. Again and again we see him getting the same effect by following a scene of high tension with a short one that puts no particular strain on the ears or the intellect, because of his consciousness that the audience needs a rest. In *Macbeth,* for example, the murder of Duncan, and the discovery of that murder by the horrified household, are immediately followed by a short, quiet scene between Ross and an old man, with one or two shrewd comments by Macduff, and in the succeeding act the emotional tension of the banquet scene, which reduces Lady Macbeth herself to a state of nervous exhaustion, gives way to a rhyming passage for Hecate and the Witches (despised by the literary, but unexpectedly effective on the stage) and a conversation between Lennox and an unnamed Lord, reflecting on the state of affairs in general, and particularly on the circumstances of Macbeth's rise to power.

When we have occasion to consider the succession of incidents that make up a scene, and of scenes that make up an act, we find that they are no longer forming a mere chain of events, like the summarizing of a plot. They are seen, instead, to be forming a *pattern*. We begin to understand what the author is intending by his arrangement of successive scenes of emotion, narrative or contemplation, and by increasing that understanding we are increasing our own interest and enjoyment. We have been let in, as it were, behind the scenes, and can possibly catch a glimpse—occasional only, but fascinating when it comes—of Shakespeare's mind at work. The playwright appears to us as that rare combination of master-poet and practical man of the theatre, and the things he is doing take on for us an added interest, and an added value, because we are beginning to have an idea why he does them. It may not be an accurate idea, but it has at least set us on the way to considering the Literary Figure as having been at the same time a human being, obliged in the course of his work to tackle certain practical, human problems, and that itself is much.

II

The Shadow of the Swan

It is not always the sins of the fathers that are visited upon the children. Their very virtues occasionally constitute a visitation in themselves, because of the standard they set. A parental reputation for outstanding merit is an awkward inheritance, as it is hard to live up to it on the one hand and, on the other, as hard or harder to live it down. That this is true not only in life but in literature can easily be seen from a short contemplation of a group of unfortunate young men who have been misjudged for centuries merely because they owe their existence to the outstanding genius of William Shakespeare and apparently fail to appreciate the privilege. When they first appeared before the audiences of their day there would seem to have been no cause for complaint, but with the passing of the centuries the author has had thrust upon him the wings and white plumage of the Swan of Avon, and his ordinary young men have suffered in reputation as a result.

Take those Two Gentlemen of Verona who supply a title for one of the earliest of the comedies. They are slight enough, it is true, when compared with the four young men who are to play such a part years later in the tragic history of Denmark; but in their own right and their own setting they are far from contemptible. One of them has a habit of falling deeply and passionately in love with one girl after another, and letting his passion lead him into rather discreditable behaviour, the other is not particularly interested in girls but finds more attraction in travel, and the possibilities of action in Court and camp. Both types are common, and a friendship between the types is common too, very largely because neither party is likely to encroach on the other's pursuits. It is when they vary their accustomed practice that the trouble begins. Proteus the lover is sent to join his friend at the ducal court. Valentine the courtier embarks on the courtly pastime of falling in love, and neither is at his best in an unfamiliar pursuit. Valentine is a slow wooer, and his lady has to help him as far as decorum will permit. The susceptible Proteus, on the other hand, finds himself transferring his allegiance from the lady he has left in Verona to the new beauty to whom his friend has introduced him in Milan. He knows he is not behaving well, either to his old love or his old friend, but he knows none the less—and says so in so many words—that he will go on doing it just the same.

Proteus has been censured as unnatural for his duplicity, and Valentine likewise for his stupidity, but it is to be doubted whether the charges can be allowed to stand. The behaviour of both young men is by no means laudable, but we must be very careful how we call it unnatural, let alone impossible. Their contrast of character and the events that result from it would not be out of place if encountered in a modern realistic novel, and it is hardly fair, then, to grudge them their occurrence in a Shakespeare play. Graham Greene or the late Evelyn Waugh would arouse no adverse comment if they depicted for us a sensitive nature drifting little by little towards an act of infidelity, while Bernard Shaw, had the fancy so taken him, could have presented a Proteus indignantly self-justifying, an ungodly blend of Marchbanks and John Tanner, and defied us to disbelieve in him until we had been a good half-hour out of the theatre and found the enchantment wearing off. It is only the unfortunate Shakespeare who must be taken to task because he has stooped from his National Pedestal to interest himself in ordinary rather trivial human beings; but perhaps the fault lies not with him for coming down from the pedestal but with us for putting him up there without consulting him.

For the two men run true to character to the very end. Valentine, when unjustly accused, disgraced and banished, has no resource but to turn to his original court-and-camp qualities, which have fitted him to get his living on the highway, just as if he were a younger son in the 18th century or an unemployed ex-officer in the 20th—or Orlando in *As You Like It*, for that matter, when his elder brother has no more use for him at home. Critics and apologists have been ready to wink at this, but have found themselves hard put to it to explain away his ready and ungallant surrender of his lady to Proteus in the last scene. The more romantic he is, the harder it is for him to avoid disconcerting and shocking us with that uncompromising couplet:

> And, that my love may appear plain and free,
> All that was mine in Silvia I give thee.

The answer to that, however, is that he is not a romantic person—at least, not a romantic lover. There is a suspicion of the eternal schoolboy about him. He has never shared his friend's taste for love-making; he has dutifully tried it and found it pleasant enough but not overwhelmingly so. It has got him into trouble in Milan, which is bad, and has apparently caused his old friend Proteus to turn against him, which is worse. To the simple soldierly mind no one girl, not even Silvia, is worth so much trouble and distress as that. If Proteus is really in such dire need of Silvia that he is turning savage and treacherous for the want of her, then she had better be transferred to him and all will be as before. That, at any rate, is Valentine's opinion. Silvia's only comment on the subject indicates a different attitude, but she is not asked for her opinion, and indeed has nothing to say for herself to the end of the play.

Proteus discovers his Julia, makes his apology and reaffirms his faith to his old love. Valentine joins their hands and is ready in that case to claim Silvia for his own against the pretensions of Thurio or anyone else. Thurio hastily disclaims any desire to oppose him, and Valentine is left comfortably master of the situation, rallying Proteus and Julia, asking and obtaining forgiveness for his men, and proceeding back to Milan with the ducal party in pleasant confidence that all will now be for the best in a very pleasant and comfortable world. So it will, probably, for him. We should take him as we find him, and not blame him or Proteus for not living up to a standard their author never designed for them. After all, he intended them to be Two

Gentlemen of Verona, not Two Young Men in Shakespeare. That, alas, is what we have made of them.

There are many others, too, on whom the shadow of the Swan has fallen, and whose true values have been obscured by it. Bassanio, for instance, and both the Claudios, Harry of Monmouth as prince and king, the unfortunate Laertes, Roderigo in a small part, Malcolm in a larger one, and, perhaps the most widely misunderstood of all, the young Count Bertram of Rousillon in *All's Well that Ends Well*. All of these are quite human and sometimes rather interesting character-studies, but we have dropped into the way of judging them by canons of behaviour framed by ourselves, with one eye all the time on their Shakespearean origin.

If we could ignore this acknowledged paternity things might be very different. Ascribe Bassanio not to Shakespeare but to P. G. Wodehouse, and there is no longer anything mercenary or contemptible about his attitude at the beginning of *The Merchant of Venice*. The impecunious optimism of a young man who is fairly deep in debt, and the enthusiasm with which he borrows yet more money (and from the wrong person at that) to fit himself out before paying court to a delightful girl, have an attraction for us that keeps us in reprehensible sympathy with him and with the straits in which his efforts unwittingly land his friend. Then we recollect that he is doing it 'in Shakespeare', which is rather like doing it on Sunday, and we pull ourselves up with some abruptness, reflecting that it is all very well, but there is a time and a place for all things, and one must draw the line somewhere, and perhaps we have done wrong to encourage him so far as this, and so forth, and so on, till we have extricated ourselves from his unedifying company and can concentrate instead upon the literary beauties of *The Merchant of Venice* as a national treasure.

Claudio in *Much Ado About Nothing* is more like a study in the vein of Sardou, a heroic young officer manoeuvred into an intolerable position. It must be practically three-quarters of a century since *Dora* was written, but frequent revivals (under its better-known name of *Diplomacy*, so far as this country is concerned) have given us a chance to be thrilled by the tension of the famous *scène des trois hommes*, in which the unfortunate bridegroom learns, or thinks he has learnt, that the woman he has married is a treacherous adventuress. The allegation is made in all innocence and ignorance, the bridegroom hotly denies it in terms that are on the point of provoking a duel, his friend calms down both parties and insists on a careful marshalling of the evidence. The three talk the matter over, and with the best will in the world the young man is unable to resist the logic of the available facts which point unquestionably to the unhappy Dora's guilt. He comes, reluctantly and agonizingly, to a conclusion that we know to be the wrong one, and in that reluctance and agony lies the main tension of the drama.

But surely this is just what Shakespeare has done with Claudio. In the first act the young man has momentarily followed his own judgement in suspecting his prince of double-dealing; he has been wrong, and has very nearly made a fool of himself. After that, he knows better and will never doubt the prince again. It is disconcerting to both of them to see Hero's dress, and presumably Hero in it, at a window by night, in indiscreet conversation with a stranger. It is a still greater shock to hear her say, before the very altar, that she had not talked to anyone at all. It is not even an excuse or an explanation, it is a flat denial, and a denial of something that they themselves are sure they have seen. If she can look like that and persist in a flat lie, which is what she seems to be doing, it is time for the prince to speak with the certainty of an eyewitness and the authority of his position. After that, Claudio may well feel that no denunciation can be too hard for her falsity, since it has left him nothing to be sure of, or to believe in, any more. The shaking of his faith in womankind is a forerunner of Hamlet's, and ought to move us in proportion, but it fails to do so because we have shifted our angle of regard and are apt to ignore Claudio and his troubles in our anxiety for another sight of Benedick and his high-spirited wooing. Audiences have changed and theatrical companies have changed likewise, for in the days when *Much Ado* was written there were no actresses to distract us with their personal charm from the tense situation of the plot. When Beatrice and Hero were played by boys Claudio had a chance of holding the stage, but in a later age even the talent and good looks of a Forbes-Robertson could make but a brief impression upon an audience impatient all the time for the fascination of Ellen Terry and the sardonic merriment of Irving.

Perhaps the conflict is one of Romance and Realism. We are apt to be sentimentally romantic and to expect an Elizabethan author to be the same, and it is disquieting and at times unpalatable to find him behaving like a realist. Rather than admit as much, we are inclined to condemn certain characters for being false to the standards of romantic literature when in fact they are being quite reasonably true to life. The other Claudio, the one in *Measure for Measure*, is denounced in our minds, and only too often depicted on our stages, as a cowardly weakling, whereas for all that the text can tell us he appears to be somebody much more like Tom Jones, an impetuous young man who has been rather too ready to treat his betrothal as if it admitted him to all the rights and privileges of a full marriage ceremony. He cannot regard his behaviour as more than a technical infringement of regulations, certainly not as a capital offence. He has a healthy dislike of contemplating his latter end, and he cannot consider his sister reasonable if she persists in seeing the matter differently and objecting to an arrangement which is possibly unpleasant but not, in his opinion, Worse than Death. It is not an edifying point of view, but the author does not ask us to share it —only to recognize it, and from the conventional standpoint, unfortunately, we do neither. Shakespeare knew better than to be self-righteous about the matter; his own prenuptial relations indicate that; but once again we are in danger of thinking that we are entitled to find nobler material in a classic and of neglecting the true Claudio of Shakespeare for the inferior Claudio of Holman Hunt.*

There is an aspect of human relationship, also, which has less

* William Holman Hunt's *Claudio and Isabella* (*see* Plate I), was exhibited by the Royal Academy in 1850, and very finely expresses the popular conception of both characters in the mid-19th century.

I William Holman Hunt's conception—probably far removed from Shakespeare's—of Claudio and Isabella in *Measure for Measure*.

immediate meaning for us than it had for the Shakespearean audience. In a community like London, founded on commerce and maintained by it, practically every playgoer of consequence was a business man. His daily life was concerned with matters of markets and merchandise on a large or a small scale, and with the question of business responsibility. It might concern the advisability of allowing a son or a nephew complete control of his affairs in Bruges, Lübeck or the Free City of Danzig, it might be seated nearer home and have regard to the company his apprentices were keeping and its effect on their honesty or industry. Accordingly he would be particularly awake to the subtleties and possibilities of a young man's dependence on an older one. Both parts of *King Henry IV* are concerned with this problem and may be said, indeed, to turn upon it. The Londoner who went to the Theatre or the Curtain in Shoreditch where these plays were first produced might have a reasonable knowledge of English history, probably from the very authors whom Shakespeare had studied when writing the plays, and this would enable him to follow the king's political problems, but he must have had a still keener eye for the personal problem of Henry's relations with his son. Here was a situation that found its parallel in every generation of ordinary London life, here were emotions and perplexities that many an auditor could match from personal experience in irresponsible youth or more recent all-too-responsible middle age. The young man richly endowed with leisure, energy and high spirits is only too ready to turn to the company of other convivial souls without seriously considering how far he may be affected by it in reputation if not actually in character. Harry of Monmouth is too sound in quality to be corrupted by his company, and the author has taken pains to tell us so by giving him a soliloquy to reassure the audience. Unfortunately, that speech has done more to blacken poor Harry's character among latter-day scholars than anything else except his rejection of Falstaff at the end of the second play, simply because we are over-ready to look at it from the standpoint of the 20th century instead of the 16th, and have gone astray in consequence.

Look at the speech for a moment from the point of view of the playgoing Elizabethan citizen and his wife, such a couple as Beaumont and Fletcher presented to us in *The Knight of the Burning Pestle*. There has been a scene of high policy introducing the king and expressing his disappointment in his son, and then a scene of light crosstalk in which we have seen that same son talking to the vast and disreputable Falstaff about purse-taking. There is a grave risk that Master Citizen and his wife (who both know what that sort of company can lead to) may take the king's view of Prince Hal unless the author does something at this point to make it quite clear that he is the hero, not the villain. The simplest method is to give him a soliloquy in which he can tell them so, and reassure them that he is going to redeem his character and atone for the time he has wasted up to now. In its way it is just like Bully Bottom's suggestion of 'a device to make all well' in *A Midsummer Night's Dream*, when there is a momentary fear that the ladies in the audience may be upset by the sight of the drawn sword of Pyramus. Instead of being a prologue delivered on behalf of the company it is an explanation given by the character concerned. The spectators at whom it is directed are not yet fully versed in the works of Shakespeare (and they may be forgiven for their ignorance of the *Second Part* and of *King Henry V*, which have not yet been written), so they may well be wondering how to regard the prince. Now, it would seem, they know where they are.

But what a legacy of scorn has that passage transmitted to the unfortunate Harry since the Swan-worshippers got hold of it! Because it is by Shakespeare it must be profound, the utterance of a great mind calling to other great minds, and therefore it must not be taken to mean no more than what it says. It must be there to indicate that Harry is a cold-blooded hypocrite, deliberately cultivating vice so as to show the better when publicly adopting virtue. The late James Agate among critics, John Masefield among poets, and Dr G. B. Harrison among scholars, have all shared this view because they unconsciously credited both Shakespeare and his London public with their own high standards of scholarship and sensitivity. Had the author been writing for them, had he even been writing for an audience at Court, or for the persons of quality who came to the 'private houses' in the days of King James, he might have chosen some other way to make his point, but he was writing for a middle-class audience in the neighbourhood of Finsbury and Shoreditch, and must be assumed to have known what was needed thereabouts in the way of explanation.

Harry's great fight at the end of the first play is the one in which he saves his father. It is a fight which has a real part in the action because it affects the course of that father's feelings. The subsequent fight with Hotspur is of secondary importance only; Hotspur's dying words indicate no change in his outlook on things in general or his opponent in particular. The logic of the situation demands that the two rivals should at last meet face to face and fight on supposedly equal terms (in actual fact Hotspur was 39 and Hal about 15, and there is no evidence that they ever crossed swords at all), but this is a matter of romance, whereas the prince's redemption in the eyes of his father is meant to be a matter of history. The elder man has misunderstood the younger, and it is only from their few quick words after the rescue that we learn how serious the misunderstanding has been.

The other charge, that of rejecting Falstaff, is likewise a grave one. The prince has shown that there is no vice in him, but that is no guarantee of his ability to take his position seriously and become an efficient king. He has been separated from Falstaff on his father's instructions, just as he hinted in the last convivial scene they had together. Still, in his father's eyes there is every likelihood that he will surround himself with all the worst company imaginable as soon as he is his own master. The thought of it troubles the king upon his deathbed and is aggravated by the prince's act in carrying away the crown, but once more, just as in the battle, he has the pleasure of seeing his son better all expectation and show a depth of understanding and humility that promises well for his conduct when he is on the throne. His brothers and the Lord Chief Justice are apprehensive, and their apprehensions are relieved. Falstaff comes bucketing up to London with a strong suggestion that he has been commandeering horses in the king's name and his unworthy expectations must be correspondingly disappointed. A good many Shakespearean scholars are romanticists at heart, and have charged Henry with disloyalty and hypocrisy, even implying that it was loyal affection that led Falstaff and Pistol to intrude on him almost in the moment of his consecration. But Shakespeare himself was as sound a realist as the London merchants in his audience, and knew as well as they just what Sir John and his kind stood for, and what such associations eventually led to. Their history books had told them that the young king cut himself off from his old associates and made them keep at ten miles' distance from him, and their experience and understanding of human nature told them why. To them, the new king was a young man in a great position; secondarily, he was a young man in history. To us, on the other hand, he is only too often presented as a Young Man in Shakespeare, and misjudged accordingly for falling short of standards set for him by a later and less understanding generation.

Two of the greatest tragedies involve the corruption of well-meaning young men by wicked older men inciting them to acts of violence and treachery. There is nothing in the texts of *Othello* or *Hamlet* to establish Roderigo as a fool or Laertes as a blackguard. On the contrary, Roderigo behaves very well when Brabantio is abusing him from his window at the beginning of the play. He keeps his temper and his manners though the angry old gentleman's language is provocative enough to excuse him if he were to lose both. There is nothing except theatrical convention—which is never very safe to go by—to justify playing him as a sort of Venetian Aguecheek. It is Iago who describes him contemptuously as a fool, and we ought to think twice before accepting anyone at Iago's valuation. When he is presented as a figure of low comedy, almost of farce, he loses our sympathy, and in consequence Iago loses one of his greatest effects without ever knowing it. If we have accepted Roderigo as a courteous and likeable Young Gentleman of Venice we can feel more pity and indignation to see how he is advised, mocked, misled and ingeniously manoeuvred into quarrelling with Cassio on the watch and at last reluctantly laying an ambush for his life. We do not see him arrive at his decisions. He demands 'further reason for this' before committing himself, and Iago promises to satisfy him, but another scene intervenes and draws our attention

French nobleman, wearing the small plumed bonnet and the richly-laced cloak, doublet and open jerkin fashionable at the court of the Valois kings, and presumably the subject of Polonius' injunction to Laertes that his dress should be 'costly . . . but not expressed in fancy; rich, not gaudy'.

back to Desdemona. By the time Roderigo is on the stage again, the mischief is done, Iago has given him his 'satisfying reasons' and he is keyed up to the act. He fails, and is stabbed for his pains by the man who has callously spoiled him of his money, his integrity and at last his life; but if we have never been allowed to take him seriously we miss at once the pity of his fall and the poetic justice by which his dying words and the letters in his pocket play their part in bringing down the murderer.

Almost exactly the same thing happens with Laertes. We know our *Hamlet* so well that Polonius' son cannot make his first appearance at the court of Denmark without being promptly recognized, associated with the duel, the sharpened sword and the poisoned ointment, and condemned out of hand as being guilty of conduct unbecoming to a Young Man in Shakespeare. That last scene has become too well known for us to see him in his true colours, and it needs a sharp mental effort on our part if we are to put it out of our minds and see Laertes as the author presented him to the playgoers of his own day.

We are given no reason to think ill of him; he has been in France and says, with all due courtesy and respect, that he would like to go back there now that the coronation of King Claudius is over. France, to the Elizabethan audience, meant the Paris of the Valois and of Henri IV, the city famed above all others as the home of persons of rank, fashion and elegance, and Laertes has been presented to us at one stroke as someone to whom it is the natural background. Four young men, corresponding to the four 'humours' of Tudor philosophy, are shown in their relation to the events of the play. In the first scene we have met Horatio the scholar and heard something of Fortinbras the aspiring prince, fit examples of the phlegmatic and sanguine temperaments respectively. Now we are confronted with representatives of the melancholic and choleric 'humours' in the form of Hamlet the malcontent and Laertes the Fine Gentleman, as the type was to be called in a succeeding age. At Court he is all that could be wished, at home he is seen warning his sister very kindly and sensibly against the danger of losing her heart to a prince who may have to marry for dynastic reasons rather than 'as unvalued persons do'. His advice is not resented, his sister replies in kind, telling him to behave himself while he is away in Paris—remember, to Shakespeare's contemporaries it was the Paris described by Brantôme*—and he takes his leave,

* The Memoirs of the Sieur de Brantôme (1540?–1614) are notorious for the frankness with which they relate the scandals of Parisian court life of the time and the *naïveté* with which they accept such behaviour as the normal conduct to be expected in persons of quality.

not to appear to us again until he comes back demanding an explanation of his father's death, and is acclaimed by the people as a potential King.

In other words, he is displayed as practically all that Hamlet might have been, and doing what Hamlet might have been expected to do, to the point of confronting his enemy at the sword's point in search of his vengeance and his throne. Hamlet could never have done it, because he is not Laertes; and Laertes is turned aside from doing it, because he is not Hamlet. The king beckons him apart, with a promise to explain the true circumstances of Polonius' death and Ophelia's madness. Just as with Iago and Roderigo, a short scene intervenes to divert our attention, and when it is over we see at once that the king has done his work. There is none of Hamlet's hair-splitting caution and anxiety to test every statement by checking it with the available facts; after one question and its answer Laertes is ready to sweep to his revenge as soon as he knows that Hamlet is back in Denmark, and before our eyes the king plays on the young man's good qualities, his love for his father, his prowess in manly exercises, his loyalty to Claudius himself, until he has achieved his end.

Once again we have seen a likeable young man made the catspaw of an unscrupulous one, and once again we are inclined to miss the point because we have neglected to credit the young man with any character at all. To us, only too often, he is merely a minor personage in Shakespeare, and consequently not worth serious consideration as an independent person, yet his beguilement and corruption by a keener intellect constitute a minor tragedy of their own. The medium by which he brings about Hamlet's death is on a par with the forgery by which Hamlet destroys Rosencrantz and Guildenstern, but such is our habit of generalising without reason that we are ready to praise Hamlet and condemn Laertes without doing much in the way of real thinking about either of them. After all, the first time Hamlet ever speaks of Laertes he calls him 'noble'; but few indeed are the actors, producers or commentators who have shown us why.

Malcolm, Prince of Cumberland, is even more unpopular, but

for very different reasons. Nobody is ever seen persuading him to dishonourable conduct, and he seems all the more inhuman for the lack of it, like a priggish Prince Hal without the relieving influence of Falstaff. Because Macbeth is an outstanding Shakespearean character study we are inclined to neglect a good many other people in the play against whom he might be measured, and chief among them is the young man who is in fact his successful rival. We are so thoroughly accustomed to the principle of succession by inheritance that there is every likelihood of our failing to realize Macbeth's chance of legitimately inheriting the kingdom. Malcolm is not an established heir-apparent with nothing to do but wait for the crown to fall into his lap, he is one of the king's kinsmen and warriors, to be promoted or passed over at the discretion of Duncan himself. Considered this way, from a passive figure he becomes an active one, a young man advanced for his valour in the field, appointed to a position which Macbeth had been led to expect for himself, and for which he might well have been considered a likely candidate. When the Weird Sisters greet him by his three titles in succession, the third seems less of a flat impossibility than the second. So far as Macbeth knows, the title of Thane of Cawdor is already held by someone else from whom there is no possibility of inheritance. By comparison, it is easier for him to imagine himself established by election as successor to the throne he has served so loyally. The news of his appointment as Thane of Cawdor against all expectation seems to confirm his chances of the greatest honour of all. He reaches Forres, is received, greeted and praised by his master Duncan; and hears the old king declare his intention to 'establish his estate'—upon Malcolm.

This is the act that spurs Macbeth to his black resolution, and Malcolm could with advantage be made a more significant figure than he usually appears, be it on our stages or in our minds. The play, as we have it, shows signs of drastic cutting, occasionally to the point of incoherence, but the long scene in England with Macduff and Ross implies that Malcolm is meant to be an important character. Take the scene as being centred on

Macduff, and Malcolm becomes tedious and irritating; we have little patience with his long self-accusation and self-justification because we know what is coming, and want to see Macduff receive the news about his children. But if we have learnt to consider Malcolm as a human being, a young and heroic antithesis to Macbeth, the scene becomes primarily *his* scene, and the position is changed, as we understand his suspicions of his visitor even though we do not share them. This fierce, passionate champion of Scotland may be an agent of Macbeth's tempting Malcolm to come back to his own downfall, or he may be a mere soldier of fortune, ready to enrich himself in the service of any invader, however unscrupulous or unworthy. Let us think of Malcolm as a human being, full of doubts and apprehensions yet anxious to do whatever is best for his sorely stricken country, and we shall then be able to appreciate his continued testing of Macduff till the latter's outburst convinces him of his fidelity, to be confirmed in a moment by the terrible tidings brought by Ross. After that, Malcolm can go back into Scotland like a liberator, winning hearts and hands to his own party until he is hailed as king and confronted with the severed head of the usurper; but our hearts do not always go with him, for we have too often overlooked him at the beginning of the play and disliked him in the middle of it to be with him whole-heartedly at the end.

As we began by considering one of the less popular plays we can very appropriately end with another. *All's Well That Ends Well* is not very often seen upon our stages, and when it is, there is a great deal of head-shaking and clicking of teeth. Proteus was bad enough, in all conscience, but what, oh, what is there that can be said for Bertram? Here, surely, is a case for arraignment and condemnation on a charge of conduct unbecoming to our ideas of a Shakespearean hero. And here again the author may answer that he is writing not as the Immortal Swan but as Master William Shakespeare of the King's Men, and knows what he is talking about.

Bertram and Helena have both been left fatherless when very young—so young that they do not know how young they are.

When Bertram goes to Court he is dazzled by Court society and the influence of his disreputable friend Parolles. When Helena goes to Court in her turn and cures the king of his infirmity, she is dazzled by the romantic situation, and the thought of being able to ask for the one thing she really wants. In her romantic innocence she asks for it, and the romantically-minded Court applaud her, but the reaction of Bertram is disconcertingly realistic. He does not like it at all, and, with the indignant selfishness of the very young, he says so. After his compulsory marriage he hurries away to the wars, with added impetus because he has been told not to do so until he is older. Once again we can watch the sight of a young man getting into the influence of a knave. Bertram stands midway between Prince Hal and Roderigo, as far as Parolles is concerned. He is not conscious of the necessity to break away, or of his power to do so, but for all that he is not completely at the older man's beck and call. He has no desire to be a libertine, but a vague sense that it is incumbent on him to behave like one, and he consequently makes a clumsy and unsuccessful attempt on the virtue of a young lady in Florence. Disillusioned about Parolles, he tries in vain to carry matters with a high hand, and at last he is disillusioned about himself, with nothing left but whole-hearted capitulation to the wife he has deserted for so long. The mechanics of the plot may be a throwback to Boccaccio, but the character drawing looks forward nearly 300 years, and what we regard with stern disapproval in Bertram is accepted as shrewd and telling portraiture when we see it in Peer Gynt. Once again we have let ourselves judge the character and the author too harshly because they do not conform to the standards of conduct that we have arbitrarily set up for them—standards which we ascribe quite erroneously to their day and never think of claiming for our own—and run the risk of following the dog in Aesop's fable, and losing the substance of Shakespeare in our attempt to grasp the shadow of the Swan.

III

Cadence and Character

The man who could write a line like 'How silver-sweet sound lovers' tongues by night' can never be called insensitive to the value and importance of the sound of words as well as their sense. Working in close association with a regular company of players, he would become instinctively familiar not only with their individual characters and capabilities, but with the sound, pace and effect of their different voices upon the stage. Consciously or unconsciously he could hardly avoid taking these qualities into consideration when writing plays for the company, and the wording of a part might well be influenced by his knowledge of the actor who would be most likely to be cast for it, and the tone of voice in which he might be expected to deliver his lines. That Shakespeare did this, either instinctively or as a matter of deliberate policy, appears to be unquestionable when one examines the cadences of his dialogue and the way in which a line may become effective or negligible according to the tone in which it is spoken and the speed or deliberation with which the words come off the tongue. Failure to give these factors their due consideration can arouse unnecessary difficulties in the production of a scene, or afflict it, in reading, with the condemnatory label 'just Shakespeare', while when they are appreciated by producers or actors, the scene may reveal in performance a clarity and naturalness that readers have failed to find in their study of the printed page.

Take, for example, the opening of *The Merchant of Venice*. This is usually hampered by a tendency of readers, actors and producers to picture Venice as containing only one merchant worth the name, so that the friends who accompany Antonio must be represented as airy young men-about-town with long legs and short doublets and a general air of leisured flippancy. This, unfortunately, accords so ill with the things they have to say that Salanio and Salarino are too often written off as irritating and unprofitable parts, thankless to play and of no particular significance. They are no more than pale shadows of Gratiano and Lorenzo, and it would seem a waste of time for Shakespeare to have put them in at all, when the other two were about to appear and could equally well have served to let the audience learn about Antonio's commercial ventures.

This is true enough if, and only if, they are played just *like* Gratiano and Lorenzo, but there is no obvious reason why they should be, and a good many indications that they should not. The characteristic tone of Gratiano is one of cheerful raillery, in which Lorenzo would join him if he could get a word in, but Salanio and Salarino have lines that become instantly more serious, interesting and significant if it is made clear that the speakers mean every word they say. Perhaps one reason for the current misconception is the change in our interpretation of the word 'sad', which ends the first line. To us, the word implies grief, but to the Elizabethans it meant sober, serious and rather dull, a sense it retains today only when used with a reference to colour. One has only to look through *Twelfth Night* to see what Shakespeare meant by it in casual conversation. There is nothing about grief in Olivia's mind when she applies it to Malvolio, and when she reminds him that she has sent for him 'upon a sad occasion', it means that she wants him to talk household business, not to go about smiling and kissing his hand and saying, 'Sweet lady, ho ho!'

So it is with Antonio. There is no need for sentimental imagination about his feelings for Bassanio and apprehension of a coming separation; he is a business man who is unquestionably not feeling his best and grudgingly admits as much because it is making him very dull company for his friends.

And those friends must look, and sound, like his equals and contemporaries. Salarino has a natural gift of expression both in his imaginative similes and in the very sound of the words with which he describes them. The comparison of ocean-going craft with 'signiors and rich burghers' or, still more expressively, 'the pageants of the sea' (taking the word in its Elizabethan sense of a great wheeled tableau in a procession, *not* the whole procession itself), is followed by a line admirably recalling the smaller boats bobbing on the surface of the water to 'curtsey to them, do them reverence', and then by the great closing line of the speech, where the *y*-vowels and *w*-sounds call to mind a momentary picture of great ships gliding through the water under sail. It is no mere butterfly of fashion who can say, 'As they fly by them with their woven wings'. The lines come to life, and gain a far deeper meaning, on the lips of one who quite obviously knows what he is speaking of and loves what he knows, like those later merchant-poets in Flecker's *Hassan,* who carry their rose-candy and spikenard along the golden road to Samarkand.

His colleague Salanio is a man of a very different turn of mind and phrase. Salarino has shown the audience that Antonio's ventures are far-reaching and enterprising on a grand scale; now it is Salanio who makes it clear that they are hazardous, unusual and, by ordinary Venetian standards, unwise. He deals in no stirring, sweeping phrases that call up splendid images of the sea, but expresses himself with a prim, tightlipped, consonantal style of diction. In his eyes, it would make anybody grave or 'sad' to be involved in such a number of incalculable risks as Antonio has obviously undertaken. Where Salarino is admiring, Salanio is apprehensive, with a strong suggestion of disapproval. (He is just the same later on, in the matter of Lorenzo's elopement.) His comments, that he would not be at all happy if he were so deeply committed himself, only just fall short of direct criticism—so much so, in fact, that Salarino has to intervene hurriedly with an intensification of the theme, carried out in his own style of genial extravagance and ending in some rather heavy humour. With the entry of Bassanio and his two friends, Salanio incontinently prepares to go, making it clear that such company is not for him. Salarino is less abrupt, and takes the trouble to greet the newcomers pleasantly and with a compliment, even in the act of taking his leave.

Once the two other merchants are gone, we get that word

'sad' again, and Gratiano gives the cue for it, in twitting Antonio with having 'too much respect upon the world'. All work and no play, says the proverb, makes Jack a dull boy, not necessarily an unhappy boy, and Antonio's claim that on the great stage of the world the part he has to play is 'a sad one' is the appropriate reply. Said with a shrug and a smile, instead of the customary

Venetian merchant. The association of the short cloak and the long girded gown seems peculiar to Venice, and would immediately 'place' Antonio and his colleagues in the eyes of the merchant playgoers of London.

elephantine self-pity, it suggests the business man who through pressure of affairs has been rather heavy company, and knows it. Gratiano replies with his famous *bravura* passage in defence of folly, taxes Antonio with putting on an air of solemnity to impress the gullible, and takes himself off with Lorenzo, leaving the merchant and his friend together. There is no more mention of 'sadness'; Bassanio wants to borrow money, and is keen to persuade Antonio that a loan would be a good investment and might lead to the clearing-off of an already-existing debt. There is no occasion here for expressiveness of sound to outline the character; it is the sense that matters, and leading players, like the representatives of Antonio and Bassanio, can be trusted to make the most of it in their own way. If they have got it wrong, from the author's point of view, that is a matter that can be

Venetian lady, wearing the characteristic Venetian *chopine*, or wedge-heeled slipper. The illustration shows her not *en grande toilette* but in the comparatively simple dress she would be wearing at home, as Portia does at Belmont.

corrected quite easily at rehearsal, or afterwards in private. It is the less adaptable members of the company who need to have the work of character-drawing done for them in the wording of their lines because they cannot be fully relied upon to create character by the way they play their parts.

With the next scene, however, we come to prose, and here the sounds and cadences are all-important, for principals as well as for supporting players. Portia has been described to us by

Bassanio in terms of extravagant enthusiasm as someone rich, beautiful and lovable, attracting suitors from all quarters of the world. It is a dangerous form of introduction, since the lady seems too good to be true, and the audience may well feel, when confronted with the reality, that she does not come up to expectation, unless the author has taken precautions against anything of the sort. But, sure enough, that is just what he has done. Portia comes before us, it is true, but she speaks in prose, the elegant, affected prose of fashionable conversation, as fascinating and artificial as a vessel of gold-flecked Venetian glass. We are not yet to see the true, natural Portia, the 'unlesson'd girl, unschool'd, unpractis'd' of her confession to Bassanio; this is the Fine Lady *par excellence*, on her best behaviour and ready for a thousand lovers to compete for her, like that other fascinator—surely her kinswoman or descendant—who charmed and plagued her innumerable suitors at St James's, and whose name was Millamant.

To balance her delightful extravagance the author has given her a companion whose wit is of a different kind—dry, shrewd and pointed. A Nerissa who speaks her lines in an echo of Portia's manner is in danger of losing all individuality and becoming no more than 'somebody speaking Shakespeare', to no particular purpose. Think of the character, however, as someone whose function is to observe, guide and discreetly criticize her mistress, pricking the bubble of her extravagance when necessary with mild but pointed comment, and she comes to life at once and, what is more important, brings a difficult situation to reasonable proportions in the mind of the audience. Her very first remark is a sententious but sensible comment from someone who is possibly lower in station, and certainly so in fortune, than the charming, popular heiress, her second speech neatly turns aside the other's kindly mockery and in seven words puts Portia to the necessity of defending herself, and in her third she has the task of explaining and justifying, in as few words as may be, the trial of the caskets, by which Portia's hand is to be won.

It is a somewhat tedious commonplace to speak disparagingly of the casket episodes, and to decry the intelligence of Portia's late father in letting his daughter's fortune depend on such a test, but it may be worth while to consider how Shakespeare himself appears to have regarded it, and how he wanted the spectators to regard it, and what steps he took to encourage them to do so in the right way. He tackles the matter boldly by making Portia herself complain of the arrangement before we are allowed to know just what it is, and in consequence Nerissa's answer, prim yet authoritative, tells us how we are to look at it. 'Your father was ever virtuous, and holy men at their death have good inspirations' goes for little or nothing when spoken in a tone of mild extenuation, but put it in the tone of the earlier remarks and it comes out like the Law and the Prophets, almost as if it were to be followed by 'and now eat up your pudding and don't question your papa's judgement'. Nerissa does not deign to elaborate the logic of the inscriptions; it is only in the later scenes that we are given the chance to hear and compare them, and to discover—if we have the wit to do so—that the trial is what we should now call a psychological word-association test. The successful suitor is the one who considers not what he will 'gain' with the gold, or 'get' with the silver, but what he is prepared to 'give' for the chance of winning his lady, and thinks that chance to be well worth the hazard of his all. At this stage it is enough for Nerissa to say firmly that the old gentleman must have known what he was doing, and that the test will doubtless be justified by results; then, without giving time for doubt or contradiction, she leads Portia on to a categorical description of her current suitors, which makes it quite clear that she has no liking for any of them. It is only after hearing her views on that point that Nerissa demurely gives her the good news that they have all decided to go home without risking the competition. Now it is her turn to raise the question whether Portia may not 'be won by some other sort' than the trial of the caskets, and this draws from Portia just the reply one would desire. She may momentarily grumble in private about the conditions, but when it comes to the point she will uncompromisingly obey them. The position has been clearly established for the information of the audience, but it is the contrast of accents and mild conflict of arguments, as it might be between Millamant and Miss Prism, that has contrived to make it clear—far clearer than it is when the scene is played throughout with the two in complete agreement. Incidentally, a Nerissa with a combination of strong principles and a discreet sense of humour is just the type to challenge, attract and captivate the frivolous Gratiano, and the scene of the rings, at the very end of the play, leaves us in no doubt of her ability to hold her own in what should prove an unexpectedly well-assorted marriage.

In one of the very smallest parts in the play, this matter of vocal cadence is quite surprisingly important. When Launcelot Gobbo has left Shylock's service, and is in search of other employment, Bassanio comes in, attended by Leonardo and other followers, to whom he is giving instructions on various household matters. After Launcelot has made his application and been engaged, Bassanio has a short final charge for Leonardo and sends him off on his errand. All this is in accordance with the behaviour of young patricians of Venice, who thought it no shame to do their own marketing, choose their own foodstuffs and send their purchases home by their servants for the attentions of the cook. Fynes Moryson noted it as a point of interest when he was in Venice in 1594, and other Englishmen who were there for business or pleasure must have seen it likewise, and probably commented on it when they got home, so that audiences might well accept it as an adequate piece of local colour. What is not so easy at first, however, is to make Leonardo's part of any significance at all. He has the one line 'My best endeavours shall be done herein', by way of acknowledging his instructions, and is just retiring when he is accosted by Gratiano, who is looking for Bassanio. 'Yonder, sir, he walks,' replies Leonardo, and in a moment he is gone. Played by a junior member of the company, the part may appear nothing, and the lines 'just Shakespeare'—in other words, lines which no present-day actor need be expected to speak intelligently.

That, at least, may well be the young man's view. But what evidence is there that Shakespeare thought of them as a young man's lines at all? Many a theatrical enterprise has one or more members who are old in experience and technique as well as in years, but have no longer the staying power to carry through a part of any size, or the memory to learn a part of many lines. For a little while, however, they can show a fine presence on the stage, and speak their few lines 'with most miraculous organ', and so long as they are not taxed beyond their strength they are still an asset to the company that employs them. Cast one of these for Leonardo, and the part falls into shape at once, a stately, elderly major-domo, taking orders from his master with respectful dignity, slightly archaic and formal in speech, both to that master and to the young gentleman who comes in search of him. More, he does much, by this brief appearance, to establish the status of Bassanio and his household. Without him, Bassanio's only known servant would be Launcelot Gobbo, and his wooing would come so much the closer, in appearance, to Petruchio's fortune-hunting expedition to Padua in *The Taming of the Shrew*. Keep him in, and cast the part appropriately, and Leonardo will serve to suggest the existence of a well-ordered household in the background, suitable to the scholar and soldier that Nerissa has declared Bassanio to be, and that was in many men's eyes the ideal combination for an Elizabethan gentleman. We have gained a fuller understanding and a better opinion of the master by this brief sight of the man.

A similar effect is gained in the first scene of *Antony and Cleopatra*, where Philo, with some embarrassment, attempts to prepare Demetrius, a visitor from Rome, for the unorthodox behaviour of the Triumvir, Rome's senior representative in Egypt, at the court of a native queen. His account is corroborated, and surpassed, by the conduct of Antony himself, with his lines of extravagant love-making in reply to Cleopatra's raillery, and his contemptuous refusal to attend to his official business. The train passes on, Philo and Demetrius are left alone, and at last we hear the latter speak. In one slow line, packed with sibilants and calling for skill and experience in enunciation, he voices the scorn and indignation of Rome, and consequently of the civilized world. 'Is Caesar with Antonius priz'd so slight?' he asks, and Philo is reduced to making some attempt at excuse and apology for his master. Demetrius makes a grave and courteous acknowledgement, and we never see him again. He has served his purpose, in showing how Antony's love-affair is affecting not only his own immediate duties but his reputation in the eyes of his colleagues in the Triumvirate at home.

Possibly it is he, some time later, who appears as Euphronius the 'schoolmaster', who is sent as Antony's envoy to Octavius Caesar after the catastrophe of Actium. An old and experienced man, who has spent many years playing kings, ghosts, priests, good old counsellors and the like, is best qualified to hold the stage with the minimum of effort and give full effect, without overemphasis, to that splendid opening:

> Such as I am, I come from Antony.
> I was of late as petty to his ends
> As is the morn-dew on the myrtle-leaf
> To his grand sea

which gains for the speaker the very respect and attention he has not demanded.

There must have been another man in the company, with very similar qualifications, to play the Soothsayer. He comes in too soon after Demetrius for the parts to be convincingly doubled by the same actor. (He may also have had a better memory for lines, as in his second entry he has a speech of medium length, which Demetrius, at least, has not.) His lines have dignity and sonority, and make an effective contrast to the light-running prattle of Charmian and Iras, but there is no suggestion of the awe-inspiring quality of the other two we have considered. A character that he quite possibly *did* double, however, is Dercetas, at the end of the play, since here again we find occasion for a voice that can make a simple statement quietly and yet with the effect of striking Caesar and his staff into a shocked silence. What he has implied in his first speech by his offer of service, they can hardly believe; when asked to explain it he puts the unthinkable tidings into one uncompromising line, 'I say, O Caesar, Antony is dead,' and a little later he elaborates the news in a speech of some half a dozen lines, finally producing as evidence his dead master's sword, the blade still stained with blood. The scene has been gradually building up, in theatrical phrase, towards the moment when Caesar stands looking at the sword—and the blood—of his old colleague, his kinsman and his enemy. It is his turn to speak his thoughts, and Shakespeare has expressed them in appropriate word-music in the grief-stricken yet dignified speech that follows the antiphonal flattery of his officers. Compliment succeeds platitude on their lips, but apparently he has no ears for either. All he knows is that this is the end—the end that must have come to one or other of them, and could never have been denied, and his words most poignantly express it.

O Antony,
I have followed thee to this . . .; I must perforce
Have shown to thee such a declining day
Or look on thine; we could not stall together
In the whole world. . . .

The speech is a worthy forerunner to those still better-known lines, given to the same character, that conclude the play.

More than one production, of recent years, has made manful efforts to play down Octavius Caesar and to present him as an unsympathetic character. For the playgoer familiar with the text it is a curious but not unrewarding experience to see how many lines and whole speeches have to be cut out to achieve this effect, and what liberties have to be taken with those that remain. Even so, with all the zeal of producer and actor to support it, the experiment never quite comes off. Do what they may in the name of originality or democracy, the nobility of Shakespeare's word-music defies them every time.

Something of the same kind is to be found in the most famous of all the tragedies. Very possibly the actor who had been Bassanio's major-domo was still alive, and still rich in authority and stage-presence, when Shakespeare was writing *Hamlet.* For such a voice, and for such a presence, an ideal part would be that of the priest at Ophelia's funeral. Twelve lines only, but a position that holds the stage while they are being spoken, and a situation that brings the speaker to the point of practically questioning the 'great command' of a king, in that king's presence. Not for the first time nor the last, the Church is making clear its unwilling submission to the temporal power. The little part calls for good acting, good diction and tremendous authority of bearing, and must have been written for an actor who could still, for a few minutes at a time, command all three. The author may well have brought him on again at the end in a different capacity, if the lines of the English Ambassador are anything to go by. Not every player can get unconcernedly over the awkward sibilants of 'The ears are senseless that should give us hearing', as the newcomer stands looking at the dead body of the king, but an old and experienced performer would be able still to do it and to form an impressive part of the final tableau, very much as did Dickens's Mr Wopsle, in the 47th chapter of *Great Expectations*, even though he was no longer enjoying star billing as a Celebrated Provincial Amateur of Roscian Renown.

As it was with some of the oldest members of the company, so it may have been with some of the youngest. In three comedies, all ascribed to the same period, we find certain resemblances of cadence and character among what we may term the boy-actresses. The parts of Adriana in *The Comedy of Errors*, Helena in *A Midsummer Night's Dream* and, to a lesser degree, Bianca in *The Taming of the Shrew* call for a player who can be at the same time genuinely pitiable and slightly absurd. All three, at one time or another, are shown in positions of comic humiliation, being deadly serious about it and just a little too sorry for themselves, but in compensation the author has allowed them to express their sorrow in terms of real beauty and to bring home to the audience the fact that however exasperating their characters and behaviour they are, for the moment, much wronged, and in genuine distress. It is a difficult combination of effects, but there must have been at that time a boy in the company who was particularly good at it.

His 'opposite number' would seem to have been small, brisk and incisive—the traditional way of playing Hermia and a fairly obvious one for the almost-soubrette part of Luciana in the

Errors—but it is not generally realized how well that technique suits Katherine the Shrew likewise. Perhaps it is Katherine's physical activity that makes us think of her as a tall woman, perhaps we are influenced by accounts, verbal or written, of the majestic Ada Rehan in the part, or the recorded fact that Mrs Siddons played it in Garrick's debased and vulgar version—in which, incredibly enough, Ellen Terry first partnered Irving, years before he went into management on his own—but whatever the reason, our general impression of Katherine is that of a near-Wagnerian Amazon. Play her, however, as a little Hermia-type spitfire, raging in vain against the cheerful imperturbability of Petruchio, and the comedy takes a different turn and moves one to quicker and more enduring laughter.

Now and then we must look to cross-references for a clue to cadence. One character for whom this is necessary is the enigmatic Corporal Nym. Pistol's fustian flamboyance is obvious enough, Bardolph carries his essential character in his nose rather than his tongue, but Nym is not so easy to define. He has been played in a variety of ways, and is apt to make little or no impression, except one of boredom with his tedious iteration of the word 'humour', and a suggestion that the actor and producer have no very clear conception of him in their own minds but are doing their best with the material Shakespeare has given them. Two cross-references—only one of them Shakespeare's—are perhaps guides to the original Nym tradition. When he goes tale-bearing to Master Page in *The Merry Wives of Windsor*, Page's comment, as soon as he has gone out, is 'I never heard such a drawling, affecting rogue', and Congreve, a century later, gives the affected, sham-sinister chocolate-house parasite Petulant in *The Way of the World* a conversational style that is pure Nym, humour-references and all. Possibly it all springs from the grave, solemn dignity of Spain. Shakespeare gives us a taste of the real thing in the bitter self-analysis of Don John of Aragon in the first act of *Much Ado about Nothing*; Kyd had already done something of the kind, more crudely, in *The Spanish Tragedy*; and from Nym, and in due course Petulant, we see how it could be caught up and imitated by people who had no natural dignity of their own. Indeed, that 'drawling, affecting' style of speech, with its vocabulary a blend of assorted catchwords and varying between the ominous and the inarticulate, is not extinct among such individuals even now.

And so the tale goes on. Resemblances and contrasts are to be found throughout the plays by those who care to look for them. The courtier-villain and the bullying-villain are brilliantly defined in the very opening of *The Tempest* by their varying reactions to the boatswain's language at the height of the storm. Sebastian's drawling patter of syllables in 'A pox o' your throat, you bawling, blasphemous, incharitable dog' has a sort of insulting condescension about it which is quite different from the explosive 'Hang, cur, hang, you whoreson, insolent noisemaker, we are less afraid to be drowned than thou art!' of his companion. In the same way, when they are both jeering at their fellow-castaways on the island, Antonio's contributions are the cruder, Sebastian's the quieter and the more venomous, even to his last ill-natured amendment to a remark of Alonzo's at the end of the play. It is not only in the things they say, but in the actual words in which they say them, that their author has illustrated their unattractive minds.

There is one other type of word-music to which we may give a little attention, and that is what one might perhaps call the *bravura* solo. From time to time an actor appears who has some particular quality that appeals to the spectator, and when the company has its own resident playwright-in-ordinary upon its payroll, he will be required to provide opportunities for the public to see and hear the actor do the things he is known to do well. He may not necessarily be a good actor; it may be his skill in spectacular fighting that earns him his place in the company, or it may be a musical voice and the ability to speak words with beauty, even if not with much in the way of intelligence. Marcus Andronicus, brother of the ill-used Titus, is an early example. He has no special qualifications of character for our attention, and his speech over the mutilated Lavinia would seem, from the dramatic point of view, to be singularly inappropriate and to delay the action, but when its verbal content is examined—and, to give it the only real test, when it is heard upon the stage in the course of a performance—its effect becomes clear, and its position justified. The preceding scene has been one of horror and emotion, the confrontation of Marcus with his niece heightens the tension still further, and at that height it can afford to stay while author and player indulge in a passage of pure lyricism. The feature is familiar in opera; we find it in works so widely different as *Rigoletto* and *Der Rosenkavalier*. In the last act of each there comes a point where a strong dramatic situation is established so clearly that its emotions can find vent in a purely lyrical passage, a quartet in the one opera, a trio for women's voices in the other, and for a matter of minutes on end we can be content to listen to melody or harmony that draws out the essential feelings of the moment to their utmost without advancing the action or altering the position of any of the participants. When the passage is at an end, the situation and emotions are unchanged, and the action can move on from there to its resolution. In practically the same way, Shakespeare chooses to give the audience a piece of virtuosity on his own part and on that of the actor. What Marcus has to say is addressed to the audience rather than to Lavinia, who is in no state to listen to elaborate poetical conceits, but so long as the tension is not slackened, the audience can appreciate the subtlety of the imagery and the sheer sound of poetry well spoken.

Philip of France, in *King John*, has something of the same function, on occasions. We remember him less for anything he does or says to carry on the action than we do for his reflection on a teardrop in the hair of the dishevelled and weeping Constance, and indeed Constance herself seems to have one speciality, that of passionate lamentation or vituperation. It does not affect the course of the play or, to any extent, the feelings of the other characters, as do the curses of Margaret in *Richard III* or that passionate appeal of the widowed Lady Percy to her father-in-law Northumberland, that makes him desert his colleagues in the rising against Henry V. It is not Constance but Pandulph who persuades Philip to break his alliance with John; from the general appearance of the part it looks as if there had been a boy-actress in the company whose *tour de force* was the expression of passionate grief or a tearing rage, or a combination of the two, and the audience had been given a chance to see—and hear—him do his utmost in his own special line. Perhaps the Adriana-Helena-Bianca player of a few years before was growing older and less suitable for girlish parts, but was now able to exert himself in the passions of a grown woman. When Julia Neilson was cast to appear in Tree's production of the play, Irving is reputed to have said to her, 'So you're going to play Constance—eh—*Crying Constance*? Well—let yourself go!' The nickname and the instruction appear to summarize aptly enough the function of the part, both vocally and dramatically, and we may not be far wrong in assuming that Shakespeare's instructions to his young female-impersonator may have been very much the same.

The use of actual rhyme is worth consideration here. We used to be told that rhymed couplets or quatrains were the signs of an early play, but the matter is hardly so simple as that. Sometimes they perform the same function as the poetical conceits just mentioned, or by their combined ingenuity and artificiality suggest an easy, leisured, rarefied society, much in the manner of Portia's fine-lady prose. In *Love's Labour's Lost* they give much of the dialogue the elegance of a dance, in *Richard II* they reflect at need the artistic philosophizing of Richard, the formal challenges and responses of Mowbray and Bolingbroke, or the dignified yet passionate appeals of John of Gaunt, while in *Romeo and Juliet* a complete Shakespearean sonnet is spoken antiphonally by the lovers at their first meeting at Capulet's ball, and creates the effect of formality that would otherwise have to be obtained by dance-music continuing in the background. A phrase in Martin Meisel's *Shaw & the Nineteenth Century Theater** expresses the matter very well in a very different context, when the critic speaks of 'the deliberate shift to a more heightened, formal rhetoric to achieve heightened intensity'. Shaw did in prose what Shakespeare so often and so successfully did in poetry, and it is not impossible that he knew very well

* Princeton University Press, N.J.; London, Oxford University Press, 1963.

what he was doing, and who had done it before, though he would hardly consider it necessary to say so.

There are one or two other 'special acts' that may have had to be fitted in because audiences liked them, and expected them from their known interpreters. The company would seem to have included an actor who had a good presence and was good at poetic and sometimes florid declamation. For him would be written parts like Gratiano, Hotspur (and, when Hotspur had been killed off, Pistol), Cassio and the fiery Laertes, but the latter would have little opportunity to give the spectators what they might feel entitled to expect from him. The action of the play necessitates his being packed off to France in the first act and not brought back until he reappears towards the end of the fourth in circumstances too dramatic for him to be allowed time or space for a solo in his particular manner. It is unwise to disappoint an audience, however, and Elizabethan audiences were apt to be troublesome if they considered themselves defrauded, so we may legitimately guess at the way in which the author contrived to give the necessary opportunity to his declamatory actor.

Laertes has last been seen in the middle of Act I. After his departure, he has the length of the two Ghost scenes and the greater part of Act II in which to change his doublet and cloak and put on a false beard, and he is ready to enter, in the last scene of the act, as the First Player, with a specially-contrived piece of heroic declamation about the death of Priam and the grief of Hecuba. He can be as effective, extravagant and theatrical as he likes; he holds the stage completely, having Hamlet and his friends for auditors as well as the paying public in the playhouse; he has a chance, as the Player King later on, to show what he can do in a completely different style; and when the play has broken up in disorder he has plenty of time to change back and be Laertes again. Even the beard that altered his appearance has been legitimatized, so to speak, by Hamlet's making an allusion to it, and after his exercise in exaggeration he will be in all the better condition to depict the grief of Laertes with the necessary restraint. It is a comfortable 'double', and one that should satisfy actor and spectators alike.

Less edifying, but no doubt almost as popular, was the special 'act' of one of the comedians, who must have been well known and well loved for his representation of a vulgar person slowly recovering from a drunken debauch. Refined minds in the past—Coleridge's, for instance—have objected strongly to the scene in which Macbeth's comic porter takes his time to answer the knocking at the gate, and have even declared that the scene must have been written by someone else. This is all very well, but the same 'turn' occurs in another play, where it is so closely integrated into the dialogue and plot that it is quite unquestionably a part of the play as written. That play is *Measure for Measure*, and the part is that of a subordinate comedian, Barnardine. In those days, Pompey was the first low comedian's part, and the question has been raised about the reason for Barnardine's presence in the play at all. He is due to be beheaded, and it is arranged for his head to be used as evidence of Claudio's execution while Claudio is preserved alive. As it turns out, however, Barnardine is trying to sleep off his last night's drinking, and will not come out to be beheaded 'for any man's persuasion', so the substitute head is obtained from a prisoner who has just died a natural death. This being so, the whole Barnardine episode is really unnecessary to the action of the play, and might just as well have been omitted. On the other hand, it can be very funny, when played by the right sort of comedian, and it seems that the King's Men (as the company had become by the time they performed it at Court) had the right sort of comedian in the cast. The Revels Accounts show that it was played before James I on Boxing Night in 1604, and there is enough evidence of the habits of James and his courtiers to suggest that the episode would have been appreciated by an audience experienced in the various degrees of inebriety. Moreover, if, as is generally supposed, *Macbeth* was written, or at least adapted, to be played before the kings of England and Denmark in the summer of 1606, it seems not impossible that a vulgar episode which had given pleasure 18 months before might have been thought worth repeating and elaborating for the benefit of a visitor from a court still more renowned for drunkenness than that at Whitehall. This time the player has a great deal more to say, and has the stage completely to himself for most of the time he is saying it, but it carries no suggestion of being an irrelevant or unwanted interpolation. Shakespeare has once more used his artistry and craftsmanship to place the scene at a point where it is not merely a piece of vulgar buffoonery, but a moment of relief amid surroundings of ever-thickening darkness, treachery and death.

IV

Story with Sir John

It has long been one of the commonplaces of Shakespearean criticism to decry the Falstaff of *The Merry Wives of Windsor* as a sad falling-off from the tavern philosopher of *King Henry IV*. What is less often found, however, is any serious attempt to analyse the difference, still less to suggest a reason for it. Yet the subject is not without interest, and Sir John's career in the pages of the playwright may well repay a little fuller investigation.

It is all rather surprising from the outset, because he makes his first appearance in Shakespeare's first known play, and has been sternly removed from it by later editors. He is named, and accused of cowardice, by a messenger in the *First Part of King Henry VI*, and is later brought upon the stage to be confronted by Talbot in the royal presence, to have his Garter stripped from him and to be dismissed the Court. The episode is a highly inaccurate version of the doings of the historical Sir John Fastolfe, a valiant and experienced soldier who had strongly opposed Talbot's proposal to fight a large French force without waiting for reinforcements that were known to be on the way. Talbot nevertheless insisted on fighting, lost over 1200 men and was taken prisoner; Fastolfe drew off his own men without joining battle and was censured by the duke of Bedford and dismissed from the Order of the Garter, but was restored to it when the circumstances were explained and understood. Later editors have substituted the name Fastolfe for Falstaff in the text, accordingly, but Falstaff was what Shakespeare called him in the earliest text we have, and Falstaff he seems to have remained in the author's mind.

What makes matters a little more complicated is that the fat knight of the later plays, the real, essential Falstaff as we are apt to call him, was not called Falstaff at all in the original version. He was Sir John Oldcastle, as is borne out by one of the young prince's names for him, 'my old lad of the castle', and the fact that in a Quarto text the prefix 'Old.' instead of 'Fal.' is found before one of his speeches, showing that someone had had to alter the name every time it occurred before the manuscript went to the printer, and one reference had been overlooked. But the real Sir John Oldcastle, an earnest Lollard who had been burned for heresy and won a place in Foxe's *Actes and Monuments of the Martyrs*, had also held the title of Lord Cobham, and the Lord Cobham of Shakespeare's day considered the introduction of Oldcastle a slight upon the family name, and made complaints about it. Shakespeare had to alter the name accordingly, and it must have seemed quite suitable to resuscitate a character who had made a brief and inglorious appearance in his first successful play, and let the newer work deal with his earlier career and habits. The company had a man who had obviously made a success of the part when it was called Oldcastle, and there might well be a chance of putting him into a play about the Agincourt campaign, so that he could go right through to his ultimate dismissal in the play in which he had first appeared. Matters did not work out quite like that, however, though it will be seen they came very near to doing so.

As late as 1611—and still, indeed, in its second edition in 1623—Speed's Chronicle inveighs against a rival historian whose account of Oldcastle as 'a Ruffian, a Robber, and a Rebell' is said to be based on 'authority taken from the *Stage-players*', and the accusation is even intensified with the marginal gloss 'Papists and Poets of like conscience for fictions'. In August 1600 an anonymous play had been published, claiming to deal with 'the true and honorable historie, of the life of Sir John Old-castle, the good Lord Cobham'. It had been performed by a rival company, and self-righteously declared in its Prologue that

> It is no pamperd glutton we present,
> No aged Counsellor to youthful sinne,

and no London playgoer of the time could be in any doubt of what *that* meant. To make the matter quite certain it included in its third act a highway-robbery scene in which the disguised King Henry V and a disreputable priest called Sir John of Wrotham were made to refer to Falstaff by name and allude both to his bulk and to his career as a cutpurse. The manager's diary and accounts, among the Alleyn manuscripts at Dulwich College, reveal that this play was written by Anthony Munday and three colleagues in collaboration, and that they were paid £10 for it, and in advance for a second part which is not now extant, in October 1599. (The date is worth remembering, because it has considerable significance later on.) The Chamberlain's Men themselves found it advisable not only to change the name but to lay emphasis on the fact that they had done so, and the Epilogue to the *Second Part of King Henry IV* promises a sequel 'where (for any thing I know) Falstaffe shall dye of a sweat, unlesse already he be kill'd with your hard Opinions; For Old-Castle died a Martyr, and this is not the man'.

Now this Epilogue will bear a little more detailed examination than is usually given to it, because it presents one or two quite interesting problems of its own. Modern texts customarily describe it as being 'spoken by a Dancer', but there is no such heading in Folio or Quarto. The speaker certainly offers to dance, and obviously did so in Shakespeare's day, but there are no grounds for regarding him as someone kept in the company *only* for dancing, especially as there has been no dancing in the play itself. Moreover, there is no Shakespearean precedent for an Epilogue spoken by someone who has never hitherto appeared in the course of a performance. In *Henry V* the speaker is the Chorus who has introduced the play and addressed the audience between the acts; in *Pericles* it is Gower, who has done the same thing, in *Henry VIII* it is once again the Prologue who has introduced the play. At other times it is one of the principals—Rosalind, Pandarus, Prospero, the King of France, Puck, Feste—always someone who does not appear, at this late stage of the proceedings, as a newcomer. We may justifiably rule out Rumour, the 'Presenter', as a possible speaker of this Epilogue.

Its balanced, conversational prose is completely different from the rushing lines of the messenger who claims the wind for post-horse and 'runs before King Harry's victory'. We must look for a person of some consequence, who can address the audience on terms of nodding acquaintance and be sure of their attention, and can not only speak and act but can, if necessary, dance. And, when we look through the names of those who are known to have been acting with the Chamberlain's Men, it is not long before we find one.

William Kempe had become an established comedian as early as 1590, and had been with the Chamberlain's Men since 1594. By 1597, when their patron George Carey, Lord Hunsdon, was appointed Lord Chamberlain, Kempe was one of the leading actors and shareholders, and he was noted for his agility in dancing jigs. As Richard Burbage was the leading tragedian of the company, so was Kempe supreme when it came to matters of broad—sometimes very broad—comedy. John Lowin, a famous Falstaff of the early 17th century, is sometimes named as the first player of the part, but in 1598 he was only 21, and it is hardly likely that he would have been cast for it when Kempe was available. It may be worth considering, therefore, whether Kempe was not only the original Falstaff but also, in his own person, the speaker of the Epilogue.

Look at it from that angle, and the speech takes unexpected life. The play has just ended, the audience has presumably applauded and the leading player has come forward to bow his acknowledgements. He is afraid he may not have given pleasure by his performance (a remark which, from Kempe, would be pretty safe to draw a roar of contradiction and applause), he acknowledges it with a 'curtsie' and goes on to apologize in advance for the inadequacy of his present speech, which he says is his own, not the author's. He must have been very sure of himself, and of the success of the present play, to remind the audience that it was not long since he had come before them to apologize for a play that had obviously been a 'flop' (could it have been *Troilus and Cressida?*) and to promise them something better that should make amends. He is obviously pretty sure that he has done so, and can go on to offer them a dance, after an arch expression of hope that he has been forgiven. It is all a very good piece of patter for an acknowledged popular favourite.

Everyone is ready to watch the jig, but Kempe has one thing more to say. If they are not surfeited with fat meat (we may presume that he is still wearing Falstaff's 'great-belly doublet', as he has not had time to change), the author will continue the story, *with* Sir John in it (cue for more applause), and ultimately bring him to a more or less unedifying end, very different from that of Oldcastle the martyr, whom the part is not intended to represent. And so, at last, comes the jig, and the prayer for the Queen, which has survived till recent times in the custom of playing the National Anthem at the end of a performance.

Shakespeare did, as we know, continue the story, but without Sir John in it, and this interpretation gives us the simplest and most natural of reasons. Shortly after the production of this play, Kempe left the company. It was as simple as that. He was one of the cast of Ben Jonson's *Every Man in his Humour* in 1598, but was not in *Every Man Out of his Humour* in 1599. In the fourth act of that play, one character, wishing another luck upon an enterprise, says 'Would I had one of Kemp's shoes to throw after you', but by that time Kempe and his dancing-shoes were packed up and gone. Early in 1599 he had sold his share in the Globe Playhouse and in the following year he performed his famous feat of dancing from London to Norwich, with witnesses and invigilators to certify that he danced every step of the way. He wrote an entertaining account of it, which was published in 1600, and it is to be noted that the style of this, and particularly of the introductory dedication, very closely resembles the style of the Epilogue. Whether Shakespeare could imitate Kempe's style as easily as he could always imitate Marlowe's, or Kempe is speaking stark truth when, in the Epilogue, he claims that 'What I have to say, is of mine owne making', the style in the two pieces is the same throughout.

If, as we may assume, Kempe had been the original Falstaff, it is easy to understand that he could not very well be replaced

Kemps nine daies vvonder.

Performed in a daunce from London to Norwich.

Containing the pleaſure, paines and kinde entertainment of *William Kemp* betweene *London* and that Citty in his late Morrice.

Wherein is ſomewhat ſet downe worth note; to reprooue the ſlaunders ſpred of him: many things merry, nothing hurtfull.

Written by himſelfe to ſatisfie his friends.

LONDON

Printed by *E. A.* for *Nicholas Ling*, and are to be ſolde at his ſhop at the weſt doore of Saint Paules Church. 1600.

II Kempe Morris-dancing. The only known portrait of the man for whom the part of Falstaff was probably written. Title-page of his *Nine Daies Wonder*, 1600, from the unique copy in the Bodleian Library.

without invidious comparisons, and it would be better to let the next play go on without him, but with Pistol as its leading comedian, and that, at any rate, was what Shakespeare did. In *Henry V* he brought Falstaff before the audience only at second-hand, in the words of the disreputable characters who had followed him, the landlady who saw him die, and even the priggish and earnest Fluellen, who had nothing in common with him but remembered him as being 'full of jests, and gipes, and knaveries, and mocks' though he had forgotten his very name. Young Lowin's turn would come, no doubt, when the earlier plays were revived, but it would not do to risk bringing a substitute Falstaff, in a new play, before spectators whose natural instinct would be to damn him for not being Kempe.

Now we can see the possible order of events between the two rival companies. With Kempe out of the company, the Chamberlain's Men would not be likely to put on their Falstaff plays, with their disclaimer of any Oldcastle connection. Accordingly, their rivals might find it worth while to produce a play, or a couple of plays, about Oldcastle that might serve to discredit Shakespeare's *Henry IV*, since the latter was no longer able to appear in its own defence. Munday and his colleagues had written their first Oldcastle play, and the second was supposed to be on the way, when they got their £10 in October 1599. Ten months later the plays were registered for publication, which very often meant that they were no longer drawing such good houses, and it was time to get them into print and sell the texts for what they would fetch. They were registered on the 11th of August 1600, and on the 23rd of the same month the Chamberlain's Men registered the *Second Part of King Henry IV*. There was no point in holding it back any longer, since they could not produce it without Kempe, and the best possible answer to the allegations of the Admiral's Men was to have it available in print, with the name of Falstaff throughout and with no reference to Oldcastle except the explicit disclaimer in the Epilogue. It was a reasonable counterstroke, and an effective one, for when a bad Quarto of *Sir John Oldcastle* appeared, after the first edition but with the date 1600 upon its title-page like the other, its unscrupulous editor added the words 'Written by William Shakespeare'. That impudent purloining of the author's name, after a vigorous attempt to discredit his work, indicates pretty clearly that that name, in somebody's opinion, was likeliest to sell the text to the discriminating public.

Matters got rather more complicated when a distinguished patron—the most distinguished in the land—expressed a wish to see a play about Falstaff in love. Within a century of the playwright's death, three different authors, John Dennis in 1702, Nicholas Rowe in 1709 and Charles Gildon in 1710, had stated as a fact that the Queen had commanded a play on the subject, and Dennis and Gildon specify in addition that it had to be ready in a fortnight. Rowe got most of his Shakespearean information from the famous Restoration actor Thomas Betterton, who would be well versed in theatrical legend and tradition, and the first Quarto of the play states on its title-page that it had been 'divers times acted . . . Both before her Majestie, and elsewhere'. This is not much in the way of evidence, but it is considerably supported by certain peculiarities to be observed in the play itself.

First of all, we may consider the author's predicament. The Lord Chamberlain's Men have lost their leading comedian, identified with Falstaff so firmly in the public mind that the author had found it better to kill off the character than to risk putting a substitute Falstaff into his next play. Falstaff in love would be an awkward subject to handle in any event. Audiences have already seen him in casual dalliance with Doll Tearsheet, and earlier in the same play they have heard him tell his page to go with a letter to 'old Mistress Ursula, whom I have weekly sworn to marry since I perceived the first white hair on my chin'. In each transaction he is so sure of what he is doing, and so obviously in control of the situation, that there is not much in the way of drama to be got out of either. He is too shrewd an old ruffian to be at a loss for long, his very character is against it—and here comes the reflection that it is not everyone who can realize that same character to the degree that Kempe did. And the play is wanted in ten days' time, if it is to be ready for production in a fortnight. It is all very awkward.

And here, perhaps, conjecture may be allowed to step in. It seems by no means impossible that a play had been in preparation by the Chamberlain's Men, with an eye to a possible production at Windsor before the Queen. If so, the script may yet provide a way out of the difficulty. The play may have been written about someone who is not in the least like Falstaff, but it should be possible to *call* him Falstaff for the occasion, and introduce him with a certain number of Falstaffian phrases and speeches, and surround him—for a few scenes, at any rate—with some of his old associates. The people who played Shallow, Pistol, Bardolph and Nym are still in the company and therefore available. There are one or two others, likewise, who have been very successful lately in *Every Man in his Humour*, particularly the fatuous gentleman Stephano and the passionately jealous and suspicious Thorello. Each of them has a good individual style—and there is that man who does comic Welshmen so well, though Fluellen can hardly be introduced *in propria persona.* Most of them have had parts written for them already in the new play, so the matter should not be so very difficult after all.

Nor is it, at the beginning. Jonson's Stephano is paraded as Master Abraham Slender, and Fluellen, peppery and pedantic as ever, is now a Welsh parson, while Nym, Bardolph and Pistol are their own well-remembered selves. Justice Shallow is rather different from the Shallow who chirruped about the old days and his love-life in Clement's Inn, and it is not clear what he is doing in Windsor, so far away from his Gloucestershire orchards. Still, they are pleasantly reminiscent of the earlier plays, and prepare the audience so ingeniously for the coming of Falstaff that when he does come, he is readily accepted on the strength of a few reasonably Falstaffian remarks without the risk of having to embark on a full-length Falstaffian soliloquy. Even so, it is the other characters who do most of the talking. With their support, Falstaff's familiar make-up, and a flash of the old fire in his first three speeches, combine to carry him through. The first impression is made, the first jump of the course has been successfully negotiated, and with the discussion of Slender's courtship, when Falstaff has gone into Page's house for a drink, we may consider ourselves back at the text that was originally in preparation for the Windsor play.

When we see Falstaff again, he is in different company, and is in some ways a different person. For one thing, he is confronted by a more exuberant personality than his own, and that is something we have never seen before, nor expected to see. The explanation lies, perhaps, in the fact that the rival company —the Admiral's Men—had had *The Shoemaker's Holiday* written for them by Thomas Dekker, and Alleyn had played the part of the uproariously cheerful shoemaker Simon Eyre. The Chamberlain's Men would naturally wish to deliver a riposte of some sort, and a very natural one would be to get their regular dramatist to write a part in which an actor could parody at once Dekker's style of writing and Alleyn's robust delivery of it. This, it would seem, is the reason for the somewhat elephantine jocularity of the Host of the Garter. When he is in full spate, Falstaff never has a chance, and can only speak straight dialogue, not breaking into witticisms until the Host has gone. And even here the recognizably Falstaffian phrases appear to have been grafted on to a rather different stock. His words, plans and bearing all suggest a gentleman of some profundity in reduced circumstances and preparing unashamedly to live by his wits. In a way, he is getting nearer to Don Adriano de Armado, the fantastical Spaniard of *Love's Labour's Lost*, with more than a touch of pedantry about his planning. He might even, from some of his attitudes later on, be a seedy doctor with an exaggerated professional manner, such as that which Jonson's Volpone affects when pretending to sell patent medicines under the window of someone else's wife. When he sends his little page away with the famous duplicate letters to Mesdames Ford and Page, he does so with a poetic phrase of a kind that the real Falstaff is never heard to speak. Not even in burlesque would Hal's old companion be given a line like 'Sail like my pinnace to these golden shores'. Petruchio, perhaps, but surely never Falstaff.

In the next scene we come to a familiar name on an unfamiliar character, and to a complete and rather perplexing stranger. Sir

Hugh Evans has already spoken the name of our old friend Mistress Quickly, and has told us, or at least told Slender's servant Simple in our hearing, that she is by way of being nurse, cook, laundress and the like to one Dr Caius. When in due course we meet her, we find that she has changed even more than Justice Shallow, being very far from the hen-witted vintner's wife of the first Henry IV play or the rather more sinister tavern-keeper of the second, who was involved with Pistol and Doll Tearsheet in beating a man to death. She is a chatterer still, but now she is a shrewd countrywoman, apparently in some demand as a marriage-broker, or at least as a go-between, but with more of Juliet's nurse about her than the old bawd of the tavern in Eastcheap. Her employer is also a peculiar character in his way, a Frenchman, excitable and quarrelsome and ostensibly a doctor but with some not very medical characteristics. Not only does he carry a sword himself, and welcome any opportunity to use it, but he is attended by an armed servant—no sword-and-buckler boy, but one wearing a rapier—when he goes to Court. He makes a passing reference to getting some simples out of his closet, but from his irascibility and readiness in sending a challenge one would take him for a professional duellist, or at least a fencing-master. And that, as will be seen later, is quite possibly what Shakespeare had originally intended him to be.

Mrs Page, in her description of her suitor, gives us a surprising and unfamiliar Falstaff. With the Lord Chief Justice, in the past, he has claimed to have lost his voice in hallooing and singing of anthems, but he cannot keep up the pose of virtue very convincingly or very long, and it is hard to believe that he ever 'would not swear, prais'd women's modesty and gave such orderly and well-behaved reproof to all uncomeliness' that any intelligent woman would be taken in for a moment. To do him justice, he would never have taken the trouble to play the serious hypocrite, because he never could have thought it worth while to try. This must be a part of the original play, and a description of the original character, be he doctor or puritan or both. It is not surprising that the author has chosen to write a short scene a few minutes further on, between Falstaff and an unsuccessfully repentant Pistol, that recreates for a few minutes the Falstaff we have always known, but with the entry of Mistress Quickly he reverts to his pontifical, doctorial manner, and we seem to have got back to the text of that unknown play that was to have been written about somebody else.

The two weeks' task, from the playwright's point of view, seems to be proving no such staggering impossibility after all. For the scene with Ford, there need be practically no alteration to the text. The stately solemnity of the consultant questioning an anxious patient will do well enough for Sir John when it is backed by the familiar costume, padding and make-up. These had become so fully associated with the part that as late as 1635, when designing a costume for a fat magician in Davenant's *Temple of Love*, Inigo Jones specified the dress as 'Girt low w^{t} a great belley . . .' with 'naked fatt sleeves' and 'buskines to shew a great swolen lege', and summarized it all with the marginal note 'like a Sr Jon fall staff'. Those padded arms, legs and body by that time spelt Falstaff to the average theatre-goer, and it seems more than possible that even at the time this play was written those characteristic contours had 'carried it away', irrespective of the very different character of the lines their wearer had to speak.

And what sort of a person was that wearer originally meant to be, when the author first imagined him? That he has something of the pedant, something of the consultant and something of the puritan about him has been suggested already. In his condescending courtship of Mistress Ford he achieves something like an elephantine imitation of Henry V, at his bluntest and most innocent, wooing the Princess of France. It would seem permissible to imagine him to have been originally designed as a doctor—quite possibly the Doctor Caius whose name had to be transferred to another character with idiosyncrasies that make him somewhat easier to identify—and played by the actor (very likely Burbage) who had recently been successful in a very similar part. Jonson, in *Every Man in his Humour*, had created the ponderous and seedy Captain Bobadilla (as he was called in the days before his creator anglicized the names and set the play in London instead of a not-particularly-Italian Florence), and on examination this gentleman seems to have much in common, conversationally, with the Falstaff of the *Merry Wives*.

As for the character now called Dr Caius, we have seen that he may well have been intended for a fencing-master in the first draft of the play, and there was in fact a fencing-master whom many people at Court would remember on seeing him. In 1595 Vincenzo Saviolo had published a treatise on fencing and the technique of honourable quarrelling, and had dedicated it to the earl of Essex. In 1599 George Silver had brought out, and dedicated to the same patron, his *Paradoxes of Defence*, in which he refers to Saviolo's recent death, and tells a diverting story about him, an English fencing-master named Bramble, and a blackjack of beer, which involves a *verbatim* reproduction of his conversational peculiarities when out of temper. These are so like the language of Dr Caius in the play, notably in the frequent use of the phrase 'One-two-three-four', and in his honest readiness to make friends as soon as the quarrel has blown over, that the latter must have been very familiar to a courtly audience, and have called up memories of the fiery foreigner who, in Silver's words, had 'taught Rapier-fight at the Court, at *London*, and in the country by the space of seaven or eight yeares or thereabouts'. Silver thoroughly disagreed with Saviolo's book, but he pays tribute to his character as a sportsman, saying that, 'This was one of the valiantest Fencers that came from beyond the seas, to teach Englishmen to fight . . . wherein he shewed himselfe a farre better man in his life, than in his profession he was, for he professed armes but in his life a better Christian'. Obviously Saviolo must have been a man who inspired liking as well as laughter, and the quick-tempered little French doctor would recall to courtly minds that fierce but kindly Italian who had taught so many of his audience the use of the sword.

The rest of Falstaff's part is practically straight Bobadilla, with none of his old, intimate confidences to the audience. That kind of speech falls to the lot of Mistress Page, and rightly, for this play is one in which the women consistently get the better of the men, as might be expected in an entertainment provided for the diversion of a maiden queen whose court was, by the standards of 16th-century Europe, a pattern of propriety. The Jonsonian style of construction, with several plots and under-plots going on at once, keeps the audience's attention occupied, so that in fact Falstaff's part does not take up a very large portion of the play, and any shortcomings will not be so likely to attract notice.

For a Court play, there has to be a masque at the end, and for a Windsor play—as this appears to be—it must naturally be a Windsor masque. Pistol and Mrs Quickly take part in it, but have lost their accents and idiosyncrasies. Sir Hugh Evans is not so nationalistically Welsh as he has been throughout the play, and is identified not by his accent but by Falstaff's declaration that he smells of cheese. Falstaff's Herne-the-Hunter disguise, his discovery and pinching by the supposed fairies, the elopement of Slender and the Doctor, each with a disguised boy whom he supposes to be Anne Page, and the ultimate explanations and reconciliations, are all matter that could be, and almost certainly has been, grafted on to an independent piece of pageantry written as a compliment to 'our radiant queen' and her Windsor court. As with *A Midsummer Night's Dream*, the fairy revels can be rehearsed independently by the equivalent of Sir Hugh Evans—the official responsible for the training, education and general discipline of the pages and choir-boys of the Household—and need not have anything to do with the common players from London until the dress-rehearsal. Altogether, the royal command has been obeyed; it has not been too difficult to put Falstaff into a farce already near completion, and such is the variety of the characters, the ready facility of the dialogue and the swift alternation of at least three overlapping plots that it is a fairly safe assumption that the audience will never have time to notice anything amiss. Then and now the spectator accepts and applauds the adventures and misadventures of Falstaff's body; it is the reader in his study who may note with regret the absence of the usual evidence of Falstaff's mind.

He ends, it would seem, as he began. In *Henry IV* he had

started life as Oldcastle, now in this play he must have begun as someone very different, we cannot tell what. And the only Falstaff whom Shakespeare called Falstaff from the beginning, even before he brought him on the stage, has now been deprived of the name and re-christened Fastolfe in the name of historical accuracy. It is a strange world.

V

Messengers, and their Function

The words 'Enter a Messenger' in a Shakespeare play call up, for a good many of us, impressions of a small-part actor in a short tunic and a hurry, plumping down on one knee and jerking out his lines without much phrasing, as an indication that he is out of breath. The important part of his entrance is the fact that it gives the principals on the stage an incentive to do or say something—usually violent—by way of reaction. Sometimes it goes to the extent of knocking the messenger down, sometimes he is merely waved out of the way and out of our notice, which is directed to more important things, probably connected with his tidings. In either event, once he has said his say, we need think of him no more.

Such is a not uncommon superficial opinion. Like many other superficial opinions, it is hastily formed and will not stand up to critical investigation. The one word 'Messenger' has conjured up an impression of boots and breathlessness, and consequently of minor players of no great importance and no particular skill. For Shakespeare, however, the word seems to have had no such connotation. He puts it down when someone has to come in with news and he has not got a name or description immediately at hand by which to identify him; but a number of his characters loosely classified as messengers turn out to be individuals in their own right, and to demand rather more attention than play-goers or producers are inclined to give them.

For one thing, Shakespeare employs them for quite a variety of different purposes. Their ostensible function is to give information to the people on the stage, but while in some instances they bring their news to the audience as well, in others they are reporting what the spectators know already to be true or false, and our interest is concentrated on those characters to whom it comes as a joyful or tragical surprise. Now and again, also, a messenger's report is employed to convey not only tidings but criticism, either on the part of the bringer of the news or its recipient, and there are times when it is made the occasion for a fairly long, highly emotional piece of declamatory narrative in the style associated with the Greek tragedians and made familiar to Elizabethan scholars by the verbose and rhetorical dramatic exercises of Seneca.

Look at the opening scene of the *Henry VI* trilogy—the very earliest Shakespeare scene known to us—and see how fully he appreciates, from the outset, the value of variety. The funeral of Henry V is interrupted by three messengers in rapid succession, and the more closely alike they are played, the less dramatically effective they are. The first one comes after little more than fifty lines, in which we have already had time to see the duke of Gloucester at variance with the bishop of Winchester, so that the duke of Bedford has to call them to order. The messenger who arrives at this moment can be no breathless courier but a person of some position and dignity. His opening lines are those of a man who is little inferior to the princes he addresses, and his next speech, when Exeter asks him 'what treachery was us'd', is a straightforward and uncompromising report, to the leaders of the country, of the things the soldiers in the field are saying about them, and ends with a combined exhortation and rebuke.

> Awake, awake, English nobility!
> Let not sloth dim your honours new-begot:
> Cropped are the flower-de-luces in your arms;
> Of England's coat one half is cut away.

It is no subordinate who can speak these lines. In the mouth of a 'professional messenger' they ring false and absurd; we know that he simply would not address the dead king's brothers and uncles in such a way, and in consequence we are unable to believe in him, or in the impact of his message. His tone indicates from the very outset that he knows the princes and is known by them, and he can greet them on almost equal terms. Presumably the author had intended him to be one of the English commanders in the field, but had not, at this stage, decided which. He may have developed into the Sir William Lucy of Act IV, who has the fruitless task of trying to obtain a rescue for the outnumbered troops of Talbot, but when Act I was written his identity had not

Messenger kneeling before a king. The man's long boots, spurs and high-collared cloak fastened at the neck indicate that he is dressed for hard riding, and would at once give that impression if seen upon the stage.

been settled, and he remained an anonymous Messenger in the script and the prompt-book. Presented as a senior officer, sent to England not only to bear the latest news but to impress the princes with the urgency of the position, he at once becomes dramatically important, coming in as he does on the heels of their unseasonable wrangling, and it seems quite natural to see

Bedford casting off his great mourning-cloak and calling for his armour as if he were going to hasten to the field without delay.

The second messenger arrives at this point. This one is a true courier, with letters which he hands, presumably, to Gloucester as Lord Protector of England and to Bedford as Regent of France, giving the other nobles—and, incidentally, the audience—a rapid summary of the bad news. Half a dozen lines later comes a third, who speaks to the lords with respect rather than absolute deference, and in a speech of passionate narrative describes the defeat and capture of Talbot at the battle of Patay and the failure of Sir John Falstaff to reinforce him. In less than 100 lines the author has given us three reports of cumulative disaster, all differing in the manner of their delivery and their effect upon their hearers, but combining to leave the audience with an impression of anxiety and urgency in the affairs of England, and especially the English lands in France.

The other messengers in the play are ordinary by comparison. Two of them bring short reports of impending arrivals, and the third would be better described as Servant to the Countess of Auvergne, since he carries no news but an invitation from that lady to the general whom she hopes to make her prisoner. Similarly, in the other plays of this particular cycle, most of the messengers are persons of no particular character, serving to announce arrivals, departures or escapes, all save two, who have a little better fortune in the *Third Part of King Henry VI*. One of them is greeted with the words:

> But what art thou, whose heavy looks foretell
> Some dreadful story hanging on thy tongue?

and is thereby made the centre of attention, so that he can most effectively relate the story of Queen Margaret's savage triumph over the captured duke of York, his death at the hands of Clifford and the final insult of mounting his severed head over a gate of his own city. The other is the 'Post' who brings letters to the court of Louis XI with the news of king Edward's unexpected marriage, and is seen later on reporting to Edward the way in which Louis, Warwick and the jilted lady Bona take the news, and the sinister messages with which they have charged him. The little scene takes on additional interest from the fact that those messages have been given to him on his earlier appearance. The audience knows what he has been told to say, and is therefore interested to see whether he will have the nerve to say it and what will be Edward's reaction when he does. The whole episode is yet another instance of Shakespeare's gift for doing an ordinary thing in a not-quite-ordinary way, and increasing its effect thereby.

Very soon he takes to giving his messengers individuality by giving them names. The courtier who arrives at the end of *Love's Labour's Lost*, with news of the death of the king of France, gains incalculably in prestige by the fact that he has a name, and the Princess calls him by it. The wording of the Folio stage direction is 'Enter a Messenger, Monsieur Mercade'. From the scansion of the following line it appears that the name is meant to be a trisyllable as if it had been spelt Mercadé or Mercadet. When this is overlooked, and the word is pronounced in two heavy syllables, the verse halts just where it should not, and undoes, by half anticipating, the shock of the news he brings. In modern productions, this is done already by his arrival in deep black, but this would not necessarily suggest mourning to an Elizabethan audience. When that play was written, black was fashionable wear at court or 'for best' almost anywhere in England. One has only to look at the portrait of Sir Francis Drake in the National Maritime Museum, or Sir John Hawkins at Plymouth, to see how it suggested dignity and gravity but not mourning. The princess is surely alluding to the moment chosen for his arrival, not to the nature of his errand, when she accuses him of 'interrupting their merriment', and it is the sad solemnity of his answer that tells her the news before he himself can put it into words.

Named and unnamed messengers in swift succession bear tidings to Richard III when he is on the point of setting out for his last campaign, and the rapid accumulation of news—most of it bad—is seen preying upon his nerves as he raps out fierce, incoherent and contradictory orders. He strikes a messenger who mentions the army of the rebellious Buckingham, and then finds that this time the news is welcome, as the man comes to tell him that Buckingham's forces have been dispersed by floods, and that their leader is a fugitive. The king makes amends by throwing the man his purse, next moment sees the arrival of another messenger who gives reasonably good news in some detail, touching more lightly on a rumour of revolt in Yorkshire, and hard on his heels comes Catesby, bearing momentous news in one famous line, 'My liege, the duke of Buckingham is ta'en'. The still more famous reply, 'Off with his head—so much for Buckingham!' is not by Shakespeare but by Colley Cibber, whose version of the play, drastically cut about and adorned with odds and ends from other plays, held the stage for the best part of a hundred years, but Shakespeare's own text is subtler, and has more relation to what has gone before. Richard's reaction is to leave for Salisbury without further delay, for

> While we linger here
> A royal battle might be won and lost.

Buckingham is to be brought to Salisbury after him, there is no time to give detailed orders about him now. That rapid succession of messengers with varying news has built up an effect of crisis and urgency, so that a scene that began slowly with the lamentation of great ladies in bereavement, and went on with line-for-line exchanges between Richard and another of his victims, has been suddenly whipped up to a pitch of excitement and ends on the brink of the final crisis.

In his later, better-constructed historical tetralogy, we find the author doing the same thing again, this time at the beginning of a play—or rather, we may say, in the middle of a pair of plays. At the end of the first part of *King Henry IV* we have seen the battle of Shrewsbury, the overthrow of the rebels and the death of Harry Hotspur. With the opening of the second part we are to see how Hotspur's father receives the news, and here again the interest is worked up by a series of messengers' reports, though this time the messengers all have names, and are preceded by the arch-messenger of all, a personification of Rumour, whom the Quarto text of the play describes as 'painted full of tongues'. It looks as if Shakespeare had got this idea from Hall's Chronicle, since that work, among its many descriptions of elaborate festivities, mentions one in the tenth year of Henry VIII which involved 'a person called Report, apparrelled in crimson satin full of tongues', and 'sitting on a flying horse with wings and feet of gold, called Pegasus'—an accessory which the resources of the Chamberlain's Men were not likely to provide, and which the circumstances of Shakespeare's play fortunately did not require. It is even possible that Hall's work supplied the poet not only with a suggestion for the distinctive dress of the character, but also with his altered name. The figure on the winged horse had been called Report, but some pages further on the reader would find an account of a Christmas festivity at Grays Inn, wherein the lady Public Weal, banished from her rights through the influence of Idleness and Dissipation, was restored to her proper station by a group of personified qualities, the first of whom was called *Rumor Populi.* (Cardinal Wolsey took great offence at it, and had the author imprisoned in the Fleet, but that is by the way.) Here the word is used to denote public opinion rather than mere unauthenticated hearsay, but its very sound has a suggestion of sinister murmurings half-heard, beside which the clarity of 'Report' seems much less effective on the tongue. One has only to look at Rumour's lines, and his repetition of his own name, to see what good use Shakespeare was able to make of it.

Once again a dramatic situation is heightened by the uncertainty of successive tidings, especially as the spectators are in the privileged position of knowing the true situation from having seen what happened in the preceding play, or, if they missed it, from the 'New Readers Start Here' information provided by Rumour. They can appreciate the accuracy or otherwise of the various messengers, and feel comfortably superior to Northumberland, who has perforce to depend on what they tell him, and the way in which they choose to tell it.

Lord Bardolph is the first to arrive, optimistically sure that the Percies' rebellion has been successful, and ready to give the anxious Northumberland a fully-detailed account of individual casualties. On being questioned, he says he heard the news from 'a gentleman well bred and of good name', and when Northumberland's own courier arrives, Lord Bardolph is quick to pooh-pooh his information and reiterate his confidence in his own version. Then comes Morton, an actual fugitive from the battle, and here again we see Shakespeare's genius in avoiding the obvious, and making his point in a way that is all the more dramatic for being unexpected. Morton arrives, but cannot immediately speak. Northumberland instinctively sees from his face that he carries ill news, and at last asks him a direct question, 'Say, Morton, didst thou come from Shrewsbury?' Both previous arrivals have reported only what others told them on the road; here is a man who may very possibly have been an eye-witness, and he gives the essence of the tragedy in one bitter, self-condemning line. 'I *ran* from Shrewsbury, my noble lord,' he says, and Northumberland presses him in vain for details, guessing in advance the bad news he has to tell, and uttering his famous simile of the sad man waking Priam with the news of burning Troy.

These messengers, then, are not just 'people in Shakespeare', or 'just messengers' who can be played all alike; they are small but individual parts that have to be understood and acted properly because they have characters of their own. It is only when Lord Bardolph speaks again, fatuously insisting 'I cannot think, my lord, your son is dead', that Morton really finds his tongue at last. He speaks of Hotspur's death as something that he himself saw, and this enables him to describe the general demoralization that followed it, and the capture of Douglas and Worcester. Indeed, in the latter part of the scene he seems to revive, to gain strength and authority and, once the worst part of his news has been told, to appear less as messenger than as counsellor and comforter to his hearers, heartening them with word of the independent rising of the archbishop of York in insurrection against the king. Where Lord Bardolph, the first messenger, is chiefly concerned to emphasize his own accuracy in the beginning of the scene and his own loyalty at the end of it,

Morton, the last, seems to have no thought save for his master and the possibility of a successful outcome, even after this shattering calamity, to that master's enterprise.

Another play, written very soon after this one, opens with an ingenious and unconventional messenger-scene, in which we see the messenger, and learn a certain amount from him, but are never told his actual message. In *Much Ado about Nothing* the messenger has arrived, and handed over his despatches, just before the play began, but we learn a good deal about the general situation, and about some of the people we are going to see, in the informal conversation Leonato has with him afterwards, and the questions he asks about particular officers. When Beatrice puts in her question about Benedick under the disrespectful nick-name 'Signior Montanto' (a term from the fencing-school), the conversation that follows tells us a little about Benedick, a great deal about Beatrice and a certain amount about the messenger himself. He is naturally easier and less formal with her than in his answers to her uncle the Governor, and speaks as if he were a fellow-officer of Benedick and Claudio, though not their intimate companion. He can even chaff Beatrice politely, at the end of their talk, by proclaiming his intention to keep on good terms with her now that he knows how she speaks of people who are not in her good books. We cannot tell, however, how much more he might develop under her raillery, for he presumably withdraws a few moments later, on his master's arrival, and we never see him again.

But perhaps the most interesting and underrated Shake-spearean messengers are those in *Antony and Cleopatra*, where they are numerous and important, and yet are often underplayed to a degree that would hardly have been possible in the days when the author himself was present at rehearsal, ready to tell them, if necessary, what sort of persons they were supposed to be, and why he had put them in at all, and where to look in their lines to find the key to each man's character. Sometimes this is to be found in the messenger's own speeches, sometimes in the words of those about him, but in one way or another the author has put it in, and it is still worth looking for.

The whole play, by its very nature, is one that depends to a great extent on reported speech. The central theme is not merely the passion of a Roman general for a Graeco-Egyptian queen, but its effect upon his efficiency—he is dallying in Alexandria when he ought to be campaigning against the Parthians—and his reputation with his colleagues in the Triumvirate at home. He hears of their disapproval, and considers it impertinent; they hear of his association with Cleopatra, and consider it scandalous. Despatches and rumours fly between East and West, and much of the action—and the passion—springs from the matter of the message and the manner of its reception.

The first act practically bristles with assorted messengers, if we take the text of the Folio for our guide. This text, by the way, has a distinct appearance of having been set up from Shakespeare's original manuscript—not even a fair copy, but the actual pages on which he had begun to write the play when he had not yet got it fully worked out in his mind, nor decided precisely what subordinate characters he was going to use, and how and where he was going to use them. He opens with a conversation between two men, one of whom is obviously a habitué of Alexandria trying to explain the general position to a visitor from Rome. He does so, the visitor sees for himself the unedifying sight of Antony passionately courting a native queen among her eunuchs and ladies-in-waiting, and is naturally shocked by it, saying so with some gravity when the procession has gone on. It is a good opening, and one might expect these two characters to appear at intervals throughout the play and to continue as representatives of explanatory, apologetic Alexandria and indignant Rome. Possibly Shakespeare originally intended something of the sort but abandoned the idea when the play began to take more definite shape under his hand. Whatever the reason, he drops Demetrius and Philo at this point, and no one ever mentions either of them afterwards. They have served their turn and vanished, presumably into the tiring-house, to get dressed in readiness for a reappearance as somebody else.

The next group of entrants contains the names of one person —Mardian—who takes no part in the scene that follows, and three—Lamprius, Rannius and Lucilius—who have no place in the play at all. Once again, we can only suppose that when he began that page, Shakespeare had meant to put them all in, found he had nothing for them to say or do, and consequently left them high and dry, not troubling to scratch their names out when that particular copy was used in the playhouse, and never dreaming that some years after his death it would be sent to the printer with the superfluous names left in.

Lamprias was the name of Plutarch's grandfather, who told him the story of Antony's having eight wild boars on spits at once, at different stages of cooking, so that there should always be a roast more or less ready whenever he happened to want it. It would seem, at the outset, quite a good idea to put him into the play, but as the scenes take shape there is no real need for him after all. The eight wild boars are mentioned, without going into details about the manner of their roasting, but Lamprias never gets beyond that one inclusion of his name—mis-spelt—in a stage direction on the first page of the play. Lucilius was the loyal officer whom Antony is shown taking into honourable captivity at the end of *Julius Caesar* with the words:

> Give him all kindness: I had rather have
> Such men my friends than enemies.

The episode, and Antony's words on the occasion, are recorded by Plutarch, and Lucilius did in fact serve under Antony in Egypt, so at first thought it might seem a good idea to introduce him into this play as Antony's friend, but it would soon have become clear that dramatically speaking Antony needed only one close and critical friend, and that friend must be Enobarbus, whose ultimate desertion, repentance and death are an integral part of the story later on. It is hard to imagine where the name Rannius came from; Demetrius and Philo could have suggested themselves to Shakespeare if he read a page or two beyond the end of Plutarch's life of Antony, and began the next chapter, wherein Antony is discussed in comparison with Demetrius Poliorcetes, and there is a fleeting allusion to Phila, Demetrius' wife, which may have suggested the other name.

All this, by the way, is less of a digression than it looks. The names constitute a reasonable amount of evidence that this part of the play, at any rate, was set up from Shakespeare's original first draft, and bears out the famous observation of Heminge and Condell that 'what he thought, he uttered with that easinesse, that wee have scarce received from him a blot in his papers'—a quality that Ben Jonson regarded with strong disapproval. And in this first draft there is a stage direction which later editors have consistently and unjustifiably altered. Antony and Cleopatra have spoken no more than four lines between them when they are interrupted. Modern editions, and most modern productions, bring in an 'Attendant', who respectfully announces, 'News, my good lord, from Rome!' only to be impatiently brushed aside by an Antony who has more interesting matters in hand, and is in no mood for business.

This is all very well, but that Attendant appears to have been brought in quite arbitrarily where he has no right to be. What the Folio says, and what, we may conjecture, Shakespeare wrote, is 'Enter a Messenger', and the whole aspect of the scene is changed. Antony is caught in an incongruous and exotic setting, being teased into making extravagant professions of love among the women and the eunuchs and the fans, all specified in the stage direction, while there is no mention of Antony's being attended by any of his own people. Suddenly he is confronted with a stern and unwelcome reminder of his responsibilities. That Messenger must be Roman, and *look* Roman from the first moment of his appearance, and the great name of Rome will come ringing out as if it were a passport to immediate audience, and a spell to call Antony back to duty. It is no mere geographical place-name; in this context it stands for Headquarters, for Caesar and Lepidus, Antony's colleagues, and for their task of governing the world.

Cleopatra sees this at once, and makes fun of it. The more she teases Antony, the more emphatically does he refuse to have anything to do with messenger or message, and at last he sweeps her away with him, disregarding the messenger with a peremptory, 'Speak not to us.' It is not a mood that will last, and next morning, sure enough, we see him listening attentively to what that same messenger has to say, encouraging him to deliver his news however bad it may be, and even to speak his mind freely about Antony's own behaviour and the way it is being regarded in Rome. As with that very first messenger of all, at the funeral of Henry V, this man speaks as one used to some degree of authority. He is respectful without being servile, and his little 'Oh, my lord', in answer to Antony's challenge, conveys a suggestion of regret without the presumption of criticism or reproach.

When he takes his leave, we are confronted with a certain amount of confusion. The Folio directs, 'Enter another Messenger', Antony calls, 'From Sicyon how the news? Speak there,' and two characters called '1 Mes.' and '2 Mes.' says respectively, 'The man from Sicyon. Is there such an one?' and, 'He stays upon your will.' Antony says, 'Let him appear', and two lines later we have 'Enter another Messenger with a letter,' leading to the stark announcement, 'Fulvia thy wife is dead.' What are actors or producers to make of this? One messenger has gone out, two have come in, apparently two have been required to speak *before* the entry of the second one, and this second messenger is the only one to bring Antony any news at all. Here, it would seem, we have Shakespeare's original draft again, combined with his habit of never 'blotting' or scratching out. It looks as if he had meant to bring in his second messenger immediately after the first, and had written the stage direction for his entry, but had then decided that this was too abrupt, and arranged for the entry to come a few lines later, after a little preparation. He ignores (and omits to delete) the direction he has written, and makes Antony, alone on the stage, call out an enquiry after the news from Sicyon, as if he were receiving regular bulletins from his wife's present headquarters. Voices are heard offstage, one of them echoing Antony's call for 'the man from Sicyon' and anxiously enquiring whether any such messenger has come in, while another answers that he is ready and waiting. It would be quite reasonable for this little exchange to be spoken in fact by the messenger who has just left the stage and the man who is just about to appear on it. Neither is seen, and the last one to speak does not have to make an immediate appearance, as Antony has a line and a half of soliloquy before the man comes in and delivers his letter, so that the newcomer is not necessarily identified with the voice that has just been heard saying, 'He stays upon your will.' In any event, the man withdraws after two or three lines, and leaves the stage clear for the scene between Antony and Enobarbus that follows, in which Antony passes on the news of Fulvia's death and Enobarbus is quick to appreciate its implications.

With the introduction of Octavius Caesar we find emphasis laid on reported speech by a stage direction in the Folio, omitted by later editors as presumably unimportant. But Shakespeare, it seems, has taken the trouble to say, 'Enter Octavius reading a Letter, Lepidus, and their Traine.' The presence of that piece of written evidence in Octavius' hand gives a different turn to the bearer's character as presented in the play. Without it, he appears to be self-righteously enumerating Antony's shortcomings behind his back, and with no explicit reason for doing so. (In recent productions there has been a fashion for making him as unsympathetic a character as possible, to the extent of severely mutilating the text when no other way was available, so that this interpretation may for the moment commend itself to the politically-minded.) To follow the stage direction, on the other hand, is to produce a totally different effect. Two members of the Triumvirate are studying and discussing a despatch reporting on the behaviour of the third. It has been sent to one of them, he is at once communicating its import to the other, and it is obviously the arrival of this report that has set off the present conversation.

The messenger who arrives a few moments later is not breathless with any sudden tidings; his first words make it clear that Octavius is arranging a regular service of despatches to keep himself informed of the latest developments, just as Antony has done with his intelligence-service from Sicyon, and as Mr Secretary Walsingham had done for Elizabeth and for England when Shakespeare was in his teens. His second piece of news, that the pirates Menecrates and Menas have established control of the sea, moves Octavius to think of Antony again, but this time to compare his present luxury with his known ability, in the past, to endure hardship and famine in the efficient performance of his work.

Once again, Shakespeare has ingeniously made the arrival of a messenger the occasion for a further insight into character or situation. Antony's present conduct may earn the disapproval of his colleagues, but nevertheless they find themselves admitting their appreciation of his experience and their need of his help in their present difficulties. How right they are is shown a scene or two later on, when Sextus Pompeius and his piratical allies are confidently asserting that while Antony 'in Egypt sits at dinner' they have nothing to fear from Caesar and Lepidus. Indeed, Pompey laughs to scorn the rumour that those two have taken the field against him in Antony's absence, but is brought up short by the arrival of one Varrius, who bluntly shatters the Egyptian dream by reporting that 'Mark Antony is every hour in Rome expected'. The news completely alters Pompey's outlook; he is determined to go on with his enterprise, but realizes that it will be a hard task to stand up against the combination of Antony and Rome.

When at last Caesar and Antony meet and exchanges grievances, we are given a reference to an earlier episode when Antony, in Caesar's words,

> Did pocket up my letters, and with taunts
> Did gibe my missive out of audience,

to which Antony replies that the man had intruded unannounced at a time when Antony had just been entertaining three kings, and was not quite himself, and that he had admitted as much to the messenger next day, which was practically an apology. Here, surely, is something very like the abrupt arrival of that messenger in the first few minutes of the play, and Antony's scene with him a little later on, and a sound justification of the Folio stage direction that was so unreasonably amended. Caesar's complaint is all the easier for us to appreciate if we have already seen for ourselves an occasion when Antony did just the same thing after dining with Cleopatra. The use of a deferential Attendant, in place of that abrupt, unwelcome visitor from Rome itself, robs the scene of its necessary sense of urgency, and Antony's answer loses a great deal of its emphasis and enormity when it is not delivered to the messenger's face.

Meanwhile, Cleopatra has been seen obtaining news of Antony from Alexas, and from her conversation with him it appears that she writes to Antony daily and sends her letters to him by a succession of runners. These messengers of hers are merely letter-carriers, no more, but after Caesar and Antony have made their uneasy truce, confirming it with Antony's marriage to Octavia, we are taken back to Egypt to see how Cleopatra receives the news. It is a scene in which the actress is given every chance to let herself go, and most Cleopatras take full and glorious advantage of it. So they may, for they have the Folio's warrant for this treatment of the unfortunate messenger. Stage directions occur every two or three lines, saying 'Strikes him downe', 'Strikes him', 'She hales him up and downe,' and finally 'Draw a knife,' on which he not unnaturally takes to his heels. Cleopatra's activities are bound to distract our attention from the person of the messenger, so we are apt to think of him as a nonentity in a kilt, a personification of Antony's description of Lepidus as 'a slight unmeritable man meet to be sent on errands', and perhaps to wonder at some of his remarks, which do not always tally with his presentation as a terrified slave. This is a scene where Shakespeare apparently wrote 'Enter a Messenger' with very clear ideas, in his own mind, about the sort of man the Messenger was, so that he had no need to elaborate them on the written page. He was not writing with a view to publication, and to being read by countless people who did not know him and whom he did not know, and who would need to have everything explained to them in case they did not understand. On the contrary, he was writing for production, and production by a company which he knew well, and to which he himself belonged. If the actor could not get a clear conception of his part from the lines, the author would be there to put him on the right track—indeed, for all we know, the author may have chosen to play the part himself. The pop-eyed, apprehensive expression of the bust in Holy Trinity, Stratford, accords well enough with a good many of the lines.

It is a better part than it appears at first sight. This messenger is no mere runner, but a person capable of something like respectful contradiction, with his repeated adjurations to Cleopatra to hear him out instead of continually interrupting. He can even meet her blows in a spirit of injured protest, with his quite reasonable argument that 'I that do bring the news made not the match', and 'What mean you, madam? I have made no fault.' Indeed, in a little while he can tax her to her face with unfairness when she curses him for telling her the truth and sticking to it. He is quite logical when he says:

> Take no offence that I would not offend you:
> To punish me for what you make me do
> Seems much unequal. He's married to Octavia.

Reluctantly enough, she admits the force of his argument, and with an ill grace she lets him go. Her last words to him, malevolent as they are, give a clue to the man's real status and profession.

> The merchandise which thou hast brought from Rome
> Are all too dear for me; lie they upon thy hand
> And be undone by 'em!

Realizing this, we are confronted with a very different picture. This man is a trader, arriving from Rome in the course of his regular round and likely to be a familiar and welcome figure in Alexandria with his news of the latest fashions, and the latest gossip, from the capital of the civilized world. That was one of the ways by which news travelled, not only in Antony's time but also in Shakespeare's. That the arrival of merchants from abroad was a recognized occasion for fashionable excitement as late as the eighteenth century is indicated by a delightful scene in Gay's *Achilles*, with its lady who cries, 'I shall be horridly disappointed if they don't show me something charming,' and her companion who maintains that 'there must be something pretty in everything that is foreign'. There is more than a taste of this, surely, in Cleopatra's rapturous exclamation, 'O, from Italy!' at the sight of her visitor. It is not only with news that the messenger has come, though it is news, and news of Antony, that she wants to hear before all else.

And this merchant-messenger has a consequential way with him. Like Polonius with Hamlet's love-letter, he is not to be hurried, even by the impatience of a queen. Antony is well, he says, and Cleopatra's welcoming of the news with a gift of gold, and the sudden apprehensions and savage threats that follow it, only put him off, so that he has to start his report all over again. This time he is allowed to go ahead, with no more than the most trivial interruptions, until he comes to the unpalatable part, and in the circumstances her jubilant cry of 'Make thee a fortune from me!' is even more embarrassing than her earlier impatience. Now he begins to hesitate, and to qualify his report with a 'but yet' that brings all her angry suspicions to life again. This time she tries to control them, speaks him fair, and asks, very much as Antony might, for 'the good and bad together', but when she gets it, she has nothing of the stoicism of Antony, and her temper makes itself felt in furious words and blows. The modern convention is for Cleopatra to have it all her own way, but that is not what the text implies when one examines it. Nowadays it is a scene between the Leading Lady and a supporting player. Under Shakespearean conditions it was a scene between a talented boy who was getting too old to play girls' parts much longer (we may notice how often Cleopatra daringly reminds her hearers that she is not so young as she was) and a mature actor who had had more experience already and was still good for several years in the same line of business. It is written as a clash between two people who, if not quite what Hamlet called 'mighty opposites', are at least a good deal more evenly matched than the conventional way of playing it suggests.

Give Cleopatra an antagonist old enough, and dignified enough, to address her in terms of respectful reproach like 'Good madam, patience!', and her physical assault on him gains in its effect instead of losing. The fact that a few lines later she says 'Call the slave again' is an indication of Cleopatra's temper rather than the messenger's social status. Once again his replies are not those of a man terrified into uncertainty, and her dismissal of him sounds like a final attempt to hurt him in the only way she really can. If the queen and her ladies are not going to head the list of customers, he is not likely to do very good business in Alexandria. The loss of the Palace custom may well leave him with the greater part of his cargo unsold upon his hands and in appreciable danger of bankruptcy, and the queen knows it. Shakespeare himself was a business man.

A few scenes later on, we see the messenger again. This time he is all diplomacy and the queen all graciousness, asking him a series of personal questions about her rival, very much as Elizabeth, in Shakespeare's babyhood, had questioned James Melville of Hall-hill about the personal appearance and abilities of Mary Queen of Scots. His answers tell us that he is a judicious man, that he has been near enough to Octavia to look her in the face and that (on Charmian's testimony) he is well known as an accurate observer. He makes a false move, it is true, when saying disparagingly of her that 'I do think she's thirty'. Cleopatra, at the time of Antony's marriage to Octavia, was nearer 40 than 30, and rather pointedly makes no comment whatever on that unfortunate remark, but in a moment she is positively purring with contentment, giving the messenger some more gold, commending him as an agent 'most fit for business' and promising to make use of him again in the same capacity almost at once. It looks very much as if he were going to enjoy the patronage of royalty, and consequently of fashionable Alexandria, after all.

There are yet other varied messengers throughout the play, notably Thidias (as the Folio calls him), who starts by patronizing Cleopatra, goes on to the point of asking leave to kiss her hand, is caught doing so and pays for it with a flogging, Euphronius the 'schoolmaster' whose dignity and reverence put the sneers of Dolabella to shame, and Mardian, who brings to Antony the false news of Cleopatra's death. (Presumably he then stands waiting, his hand demurely extended for a gratuity, since Antony tells him roundly that it is payment enough to let him go away alive.) *Antony and Cleopatra* is the most messenger-ridden play of the whole Shakespearean canon, and the best possible illustration of the author's versatility in handling the process of conveying information, whether to the mimic Romans in the acting-area or to the very genuine Jacobean Londoners in the pit or galleries at the Globe.

VI

Problem Play

The average Elizabethan with a grievance had various ways in which he might air it, though they were not all of them very safe ones. Perhaps the best was to publish a pamphlet with an arresting title, and see to its distribution in the right quarter. It would be well to avoid anything that could be construed as treason, however; a puritan named John Stubbes had had his right hand struck off in public for bringing out a tract that denounced the queen's projected marriage to the duke of Anjou. One could also descend to a rather lower level and assail one's opponents by following Falstaff's threat of 'having ballads made on you all and sung to filthy tunes', or if the offence were a social rather than a political one, it might be possible to interest a preacher in it, with a view to a spirited denunciation from the pulpit. What one would *not* expect to find is a social abuse or convention attacked or criticized in a play by Shakespeare. Jonson, perhaps—especially if it involved the personality of someone with whom he had lately and violently quarrelled—but not Shakespeare. It seems completely out of keeping with what we can guess of his appearance and personality, and what we can learn about his reputation among his contemporaries and his position and responsibilities at the Globe. Yet there is one play in which he seems to have done that very thing, and provided, in almost Ibsenite manner, a presentation of a state of affairs which needed examination, criticism and, if possible, amendment.

That play is *All's Well that Ends Well,* and we are fortunate in having an unusually helpful amount of source-material to guide us in tracing its development. For many years it has been considered an unsatisfactory play, with a most unheroic hero who cuts a very poor figure beside, in Shaw's expressive phrase, 'his enlightened lady doctor wife'. What its critics have lost sight of, or have never realized, is that Bertram's character, in the days when the play was new, would be accepted as the result of a state of things with which a good many people were becoming increasingly dissatisfied. Comparison of the original Boccaccio story—the ninth *novella* of the third day of the *Decameron* —with Shakespeare's treatment of it will show, not only that he elaborated the opening scene and some of the motivation, but that he did so in accordance with opinions that were very strongly held in certain quarters and had been ventilated in more than one publication before he himself was born.

Boccaccio wrote the original story in the Middle Ages, *about* the Middle Ages, and to him and to his readers, accordingly, it was a natural thing, acceptable without comment or question, that a young man who inherited an estate while still under age should become a ward of his feudal overlord, and that a king should offer a suitable marriage as a reward for good service, like that later Lord Chancellor who claimed to

> sit all day
> Giving agreeable girls away,

when introducing himself in the first act of *Iolanthe*. By the time Shakespeare wrote, however, things were very different. As he handles the story, it has nothing of the Middle Ages about it. The soldiers are obviously serving in a Renaissance army, and the court of France is depicted unmistakably as a Renaissance court, and in the court of the Valois that particular piece of feudalism did not, by then, exist. But—and this is the important point—in England it still did, and was by no means generally approved of. (All the same, it was not abolished here until the Restoration of Charles II.)

Professor Joel Hurstfield has shown us, in *The Queen's Wards* and elsewhere, why the custom was not discontinued earlier. As with many other abuses, both before and since, it made a very comfortable income for somebody, at the expense of people who were not of an age, or in a position, to complain. An heir or heiress of land held under knight-service, who became while still a minor, a ward of its overlord, could be married off at that overlord's pleasure or discretion as arbitrarily as at a parent's. What was more regrettable was that these marriages could be, and often were, arranged on a business basis to a scandalous degree. An enterprising financier might buy the wardship of an heir or heiress with a view to ultimately marrying off the ward to a member of his own family or, quite simply and unashamedly, to the highest bidder. Sir Nicholas Bacon had been Attorney to the Court of Wards in 1546, and had expressed uncompromising disapproval of the system. Sir Thomas Smith, nearly twenty years later, had complained that young men who had been wards were apt to be ill-bred and ill-educated because their guardians-by-purchase were not concerned to spend much money on them, and that being married very young they 'many times do not love their wives'. Matters must have improved somewhat when the Mastership of the Court of Wards was held by such a figure of integrity as William Cecil, Lord Burghley, and it is known that he himself was most conscientious in his duty to his own personal wards, but the fact remained that the whole thing was a mediaeval survival and had a good deal to be said against it.

With this in mind, we can turn to the play with renewed interest, and see how Shakespeare handled the original story in the light of the more recent reading on the subject. He may not necessarily have felt very strongly about it, but we can make a guess, from some of his other plays, how he customarily went about his task. In the best of the Histories, it seems that he got his general ideas from Hall's Chronicle, then looked up the same episodes in Holinshed and others, for any extra details, and worked the best of all of them into his text. It is easy to imagine him doing so here. The Boccaccio story he would have met in its English translation in Painter's *Palace of Pleasure*, which came out in 1566. When considering it for dramatic purposes, he might well think it advisable to look up the details of wardship in any available publications, since the plot turned upon them at an important point, and he would find that the published material was inclined to be somewhat critical in a way germane to the story and the development of the characters.

From the outset he takes care not to present the system as

iniquitous, or the guardian of the wards as a callous and unscrupulous money-getter. On the contrary, the first three speeches of the play set forth quite clearly both the opening situation and the way in which the spectators are to regard it. The visual effect is indicated by the stage direction in the Folio, 'Enter yong Bertram Count of Rossillion, his Mother, and Helena, Lord Lafew, all in blacke,' and the old Countess, in the most natural way in the world, informs the audience of the position by her opening words to Lord Lafeu, 'In delivering my son from me, I bury a second husband.' Bertram, in his turn, adds a further piece of information when he says, 'I must attend his Majesty's command, to whom I am now in ward, evermore in subjection.' Lafeu tries to cheer them both with assurances of the king's kindness and consideration, particularly to people of such merit as theirs. Only when the important points of the situation have been made perfectly clear in this way does the conversation move to the secondary subjects of the king's illness and the medical skill of Helena's lately-deceased father. All these points, by the way, are made in clear and comprehensible prose. There is to be no risk of distracting the audience by the music of Shakespeare's verse so that they miss this very 'necessary question of the play'. Accordingly, the poetic element is kept back until Bertram kneels before his mother for her blessing as he takes his leave. After that, it is given free rein in Helena's outburst when she is momentarily alone, and again when, in her conversation with Parolles, she lets her mind dwell on Bertram's opportunities at Court.

With the next scene, we are at that same court, and the verse takes on the dignity and sonority of the Roman scenes in *Antony and Cleopatra*. After a flourish of trumpets, the king of France enters 'with Letters, and divers attendants', and concerns himself at once with business of state, refusing to be drawn into war in Italy but giving leave to such French gentlemen as wish to serve as volunteers in support either of Florence or of her adversary Siena. Bertram is presented and graciously received, with a compliment, a welcome and a passage of kindly remembrance of his dead father. There is no suggestion of carelessness or avarice; in this short scene the king is presented to us as a grave, courteous figure, conscientiously carrying out his responsibilities in the face of crippling ill-health and a tormenting sense of his own inadequacy because of it. We get a further detail of information at the very end of the scene, when we learn that Helena's father has been dead for six months, and the king's reference to him bears out what old Lafeu has already said about his high reputation; then with another flourish the king goes wearily away, leaning on an attendant's arm, and with a kindly word to Bertram he leaves him.

The prose scene that follows gives us another survival of feudalism, slightly caricaturing the first one, since the Clown, being a vassal of Rousillon, has to apply to the old Countess for permission to marry. His conversation with her is the kind of semi-smart exchange that Shakespeare had done before, and done better, in *Twelfth Night*. We may suppose that a clown such as Robert Armin did this sort of thing well, and audiences liked it, so that it was as well to give him a suitable opportunity now and then, but it went out of fashion in the next reign, and by 1647 we find William Cartwright roundly saying that, in comparison with Beaumont and Fletcher, Shakespeare was dull and rather vulgar,

> whose best jest lies
> I'th'Lady's questions, and the Fool's replies.

Once again, a prose scene turns to pure lyricism when a character is left alone upon the stage, very much as in a later type of romance a scene of back-chat with a leading comedian is followed by a serious musical 'number'. The Countess, when alone, speaks not only in verse, but in rhyme—an eight-line stanza consisting of a quatrain and two couplets—and the succeeding scene with Helena is played in verse that makes the most of its dramatic tension and the warmth of affection felt by both parties.

So far, there seems to be nothing for Bertram to complain about, in his position as a royal ward, but the opening of the next act introduces one of the charges made against the system. Some of the French lords have availed themselves of the royal permission to fight in the Italian war as volunteers, and are come to take their leave of the king before doing so, but Bertram is not allowed to be one of them, and is indignant, to his hanger-on Parolles, about being 'commanded here, and kept a coil with'. The trouble was that immature heirs to great estates were valuable people who needed careful looking-after and must not be allowed to run risks—not, at least, until their marriages had been brought about, with suitable settlements to the profit of their guardians. Sir Humphrey Gilbert, who worked out a detailed scheme for the better education of such young unfortunates, made a point of the fact that they were 'estranged from all serviceable virtues to their prince and country' such as that spell of military service, under a reputable commander, that was usually thought to be such good training for a young man of rank. With some ingenuity, Shakespeare makes Bertram chafe at the restriction, and resolve to steal away from Paris, at this early stage, while one of the older lords who are going is still there to hear and applaud the project. Bertram's traducers have been so ready to expatiate on his flight to Italy as a refuge from an unwanted marriage that it is worth while to remember that he first embraced the idea for a far nobler reason, and earned commendation for it from a person of judgement, before the other question came up at all.

Now comes the fine scene in which old Lafeu brings Helena before the sick king and she succeeds in persuading him to accept her treatment. As the king has had enough of new physicians and new prescriptions, and has given up hope of getting advantage from any of them, the astute old nobleman plays on his curiosity by his exaggerated praise of the visitor he has brought with him. The king cannot resist the temptation to see, at least, what sort of person has roused Lafeu to these extravagances, and Helena —suddenly bashful and reluctant, on attaining the interview she has hoped for—is brought in. It is interesting to see how gracefully the author passes from blank verse to rhymed couplets as the conversation develops from spontaneous assertion of opinion on one side and the other to a degree of measured, careful argument which the king finds increasingly hard to counter. Once again, a scene that has started by being dramatic has now become almost musical into the bargain. The couplets are not the ingeniuous jingle of a Victorian pantomime-text or one of the tours-de-force that Planché contrived for the Vestris management at the Olympic; they give a foretaste of the music of the best work of Dryden in the way they lift a scene to a different plane of nobility, and give the characters an appearance of being a little larger than life. By this ingenuity, Helena's request for a husband of the king's bestowing comes across like the sentence of a goddess or a prophetess, and carries with it no suggestion of the marriage-market conducted by the guardians of wards upon occasion, even though she specifically reassures the king that she will ask only for one

> thy vassal, whom I know
> Is free for me to ask, thee to bestow.

Such, obviously, must the young men be who are paraded for Helena's inspection and selection when she has made good her claim and the late invalid is now 'able to lead her a coranto'. This is an important point. The lords are all young, rich and sure that their destiny is to be married off in due course to someone selected by the king for considerations that have nothing to do with their own feelings. They may well be somewhat apprehensive about it, and ready to welcome the chance of marriage with the present candidate, who is young, personable and obviously in great favour with the king. Quite apart from his ominous remark that 'Who shuns thy love shuns all his love in me', there must be a general impression that the man who gets her will have done very well for himself. The verse takes on the formal stateliness of couplets as Helena moves from one lord to the next, with a compliment for each and a verdict which comes to each as a disappointment, while Lafeu looks on and grumbles indignantly—in prose—on What Young Men are Coming To. Finally she comes to the last in the line, the one most newly come to Court from the depths of the country, and lays all badinage aside with a phrase of moving simplicity:

> I dare not say I take you, but I give
> Me and my service, ever whilst I live
> Into your guiding power. *This* is the man!

She has given to an obscure young man the greatest compliment she can bestow, and what the unsuccessful candidates would consider the best possible chance of further advancement in the king's favour, but the young man in question is so unappreciative as to recoil from the idea, with words that are both insubordinate to the king and discourteous to the lady. It is quite clear that he is so young, and so ignorant of his position and obligations, that he has never realized the full implication of his earlier light remark about being 'now in ward, evermore in subjection' to his royal guardian. He keeps on asking for freedom of choice, or for an explanation—to neither of which is he entitled—and the king, with considerable restraint, explains once more his own indebtedness to Helena. The one point which Bertram might have made, but has not had the knowledge or the intelligence to make, is that a ward should be given in marriage to someone of his or her social standing, and the king makes this point himself. Bertram's unwisely scornful remark about 'a poor physician's daughter' is taken up and cuttingly echoed by the king, who goes on to point out the nature of true honour—the use of rhyme here helps to show that he is obliged to seem sententious and to remind Bertram of principles that should have needed no explanation—and finally declares that it is for himself, as the fountain of honour, to bestow rank and fortune where he thinks fit.

Bertram's answer, 'I cannot love her, nor will strive to do it,' is that of a naughty child that knows itself to be in the wrong, and draws down on him an instant snub from the king. Poor Helena, by this time, is distressed and embarrassed by the storm that she has unwittingly called up. She tries to calm it by withdrawing her request, but matters have gone too far for that. The king has given his word and must honour it, if necessary by the exercise of his authority. Bertram is roundly told to obey orders or take the consequences, and though his agreement is so ungraciously abject as to be an insult in itself, the king ignores its tone and promises to dower the bride on a scale that will equal Bertram's own estate, if indeed it does not surpass it. A short scene between Parolles and Lafeu follows, and when Bertram reappears he is married, resentful and determined to send his wife home at once and go off himself to the Italian wars, a wedding-present from the king having supplied him with the means. The course of the story has broadly followed Boccaccio, but Shakespeare's handling of it has brought out more emphatically the points raised by Sir Thomas Smith and his fellow-objectors to the wardship system. Bertram is shown as being very young, self-centred, childish and instinctively hostile to his wife, just as Sir Thomas had specified, and we learn from a remark by Parolles that he has acted in a still more ungentlemanly manner by telling Helena to ask the king for leave to return home at once, so as to create the impression that the withdrawal from court is done at her request and not her husband's.

So far has Shakespeare gone to show Bertram at his worst that he runs the risk of invalidating his argument by making it seem that it is the young man's nature, and not the system, that is causing all the trouble. At this point, accordingly, he seems to be doing something to restore the balance. When Lafeu tries to warn him against the company he is keeping in associating with the awful Parolles, Bertram is hot in defence of his friend, but at the same time, when the older man has gone, is not very ready to accept Parolles' light dismissal of him as 'an idle lord'. Confronting Helena again he speaks to her apologetically, almost kindly, and his halting replies to her leave-taking suggest that he is in the not uncommon state of feeling very properly ashamed of what he is doing but determined to persist in doing it all the same, particularly with Parolles to urge him on.

At this stage the play abandons social criticism in favour of military farce, in the course of which we are given a new and encouraging sidelight on Bertram as a soldier, since he has served with distinction in the campaign against the Sienese. When his brother-officers in their turn insist on the cowardice and depravity of Parolles, he at last agrees to take part with them in a practical joke to test the man's valour, and is given

An army encampment in its leisure moments. This is exactly the type of life depicted in Acts III and IV of *All's Well that Ends Well*, even to the drum lying in the middle distance.

embarrassing but incontrovertible proof when Parolles, bound, blindfolded and believing that he is undergoing interrogation by the enemy, pours out answers to all the questions asked him about the strength of the Florentine army in cavalry and infantry, its general morale and the character and morals of various individual officers, including Bertram himself. This episode is not in the Boccaccio story, but makes a brilliant foil to the more relevant event in this act, namely the substitution of the disguised Helena for Diana, the Florentine lady whom Bertram has been somewhat ineffectively trying to seduce.

With the final act we are back in France, and Shakespeare is back on the theme of wardship and its drawbacks. Once more he displays a masterly talent for exhibiting his characters at their best while on the point of doing something that we cannot approve of, and that he does not intend us to approve of. The king shows himself properly grieved for the supposedly dead Helena, gracious and sympathetic to the countess and magnanimous to Bertram, who is to be received without having to sue for readmission to the royal favour. As far as can be, his master has 'forgiven and forgotten all'. He has had letters reporting on Bertram's good service abroad, and the words of all the characters predispose us, when Bertram reappears, to receive him back into our good graces as he is being received into the king's. Half a line from Lafeu serves to indicate, also, that he is looking his best, and his first action on entering is to ask, in very proper terms, for his sovereign's forgiveness.

And then, just as everything has got to this stage, the trouble begins again. Bertram, still under age and now a widower, has gone back into stock as a marriageable ward and is available for issue to someone else. This time it is to a daughter of Lafeu; Bertram frankly admits that he has admired her in the past, and that it was his admiration for her that led him to undervalue Helena. The system is being put into operation again, and this time he is prepared to obey instructions. He is asked to send a token to his new betrothed, and hands over a ring which he got in Italy, and which can hardly, therefore, have any associations at home. To his surprise and horror, all sorts of people seem to be recognizing it and, what is worse, associating it with Helena, which is quite impossible, since he very well knows it was given to him, in exchange for his family signet, by a young woman called Diana in the course of a night assignation in Florence. Yet Lafeu says he saw Helena wear it, his own mother says the same and adds that she valued it 'at her life's rate', and the king clinches the matter by saying categorically that it was he himself who gave it her, with instructions to use it in applying to him if ever she should need help. The young man who has won himself a name for skill and bravery in battle is suddenly revealed as very young indeed, and in his bewilderment and panic he begins to lie as wildly and fantastically as Parolles himself. The king is not impressed, and Bertram has to reiterate his earlier asseveration—in the truth of which, of course, he passionately believes—that 'she never saw it'.

This line of defence is the worst that can be imagined. In view of the king's knowledge of the ring, the purpose for which he gave it to Helena, the countess's tribute to the value Helena set on it, and the fact that it has been found in Bertram's possession and causes him considerable uneasiness, the matter begins to have a very ugly look, as if there had been foul play somewhere. The king orders Bertram's arrest, and the young man is taken away under guard, protesting his innocence in terms that the audience, but not the king and those with him, can recognize as an unwittingly accurate representation of the facts. Diana's letter is now brought in, with its tale of Bertram's attempt on her virtue in Florence, and we have a little touch of the marriage-market in Lafeu's reception of the information, since he roundly declares himself ready to pay a forfeit rather than accept the son-in-law that the king has offered him. The king, on the other hand, congratulates Lafeu on a narrow escape, sends for Bertram again to confront him with Diana, and says outright that he fears Helena has been murdered. He says it almost apologetically to the countess, as it is quite clear that if murder has been done, Bertram is the most likely person to have done it, and it is typical of the old lady's combined loyalty and integrity that she can at once make a reply that tries neither to accuse nor to defend her son.

'Now, justice on the doers,' she says, making it clear that the person who really matters is Helena, the one who has been wronged.

These complications, and the return of the king, are all Shakespeare's, not Boccaccio's, and properly used they can give the play a balance that is sometimes overlooked. The point is that by this time Bertram is really in peril of his life. It is not a matter now of deserting a wife or leaving the court without permission, or seducing an orphan girl abroad, but one of murder, and murder for a very unsavoury motive. The king is angry, the evidence is very suggestive, and Bertram's own conduct under examination is putting him in a very bad light, and as a result the spectators, who know that unsatisfactory as his behaviour has been, he is not in fact a murderer, are better disposed to regard him with some degree of sympathy. There is something to be said for being unjustly accused, so long as one can finally demonstrate that the accusation *was* an unjust one, and this is Shakespeare's way of bringing Bertram some way back into our good graces.

He has a lot to go through first, however. Faced with a living and accusing Diana, whom he believes he has wronged, and driven frantic by suggestions about a presumably dead Helena, whom he knows he has not murdered but cannot prove it, he falls back again on wild and unfounded allegations. There is nothing more about a noble lady throwing him a ring out of a casement in hopeless love for him; first he tries to brazen things out and call Diana merely 'a fond and desperate creature' then he slanders her more grossly as having been 'a common gamester to the camp', but this draws down on him a damning piece of evidence, the production of the ancient family ring which he had no business to give away to anyone. Last of all, when he hears that Parolles is to be brought in evidence against him, he falls back on what he believes to be the truth.

Now it is Diana's turn to be so enigmatical in her replies that the king orders her arrest and threatens her with death unless she reveals where she obtained Helena's ring. She chooses to 'put in bail', and sends out her mother to return—to everybody's stupefaction—with the lost Helena, unquestionably alive, and claiming to have fulfilled Bertram's petulant, supposedly impossible conditions. He has given her his ring, and she is about to bear his child, and he is at her feet pleading for pardon. Even now, the actor can give a wrong impression if he speaks his last couplet in the wrong way.

> If she, my liege, can make me know this clearly,
> I'll love her dearly, ever, ever dearly

must not come out judicially, as if it were to be followed by the words 'but not otherwise'. Bertram has been scared to the verge of frenzy with the possibility of being executed for a murder which he has not committed, and direct accusation of a seduction which he thought he had committed but now finds that somehow he has not, he has had brought home to him the true worth of a wife he had treated very badly, and he can hardly tell, by this time, what has really happened. The one person, it seems, who can explain everything is the much injured but apparently still loving Helena, and it is to her, even while addressing the king, that he appeals for that explanation, of which he is in such desperate need.

All is well ended, says the playwright, but if so, it is no thanks to the system, which has done pretty well all the things objected against it by other people. Perhaps it is a sign of grace in the king that at the last moment he does not produce a ready-made husband for Diana but promises instead to give her a dowry when she has chosen a husband for herself. We may wonder, perhaps, whether there was some recent case of a ward unsuitably married in the early years of James I that had brought the subject up into public interest. The general style of the play suggests a date of 1605–1608 or so, and Shakespeare's colleague George Wilkins produced *The Miseries of Enforced Marriage* in 1607, so perhaps the subject was a topical one. At any rate, it is interesting to see how closely Shakespeare himself follows the main charges made by Sir Thomas Smith and others, while in his drawing of Bertram, and still more in the king, he contrives to show that the trouble is not the fault of the people concerned, but of the anachronism which they have to operate, or which does its part, by its influence, to make them what they are.

VII

A Sentence in Hall

Whenever the question of Shakespeare's sources comes up for discussion we hear a good deal about Raphael Holinshed and his Chronicle, and there is even a certain amount of hair-splitting about which edition he consulted, but little or nothing is said about Edward Hall, on whose work Holinshed drew so freely. This is a grave omission, because from the historical standpoint Hall is the more important of the two. Holinshed was an editor rather than an author; he was employed by a publisher from Strasburg called Reyner Wolfe, for whom he skilfully collated the published writings of several earlier historians into a more or less continuous narrative, with due acknowledgements, in the margin, to his various sources. Wolfe had engaged William Harrison to write an introductory 'Description' of England and its institutions from a geographical and social point of view, and Holinshed duly brought the historical part up to date by adding an Elizabethan section. The result was an encyclopaedic account of the British Isles from the earliest times, first published in 1577 with a host of spirited but largely irrelevant illustrations, and reprinted, with an augmented text but no pictures, in 1587. From Holinshed, unquestionably, Shakespeare got his material for the semi-legendary stories of Macbeth, Cymbeline and King Lear, and certain odd details for his main series of historical plays, but the general form of that series, and quite possibly the original conception of it, can be attributed to an earlier source, and one which the poet could have known from his early boyhood.

Hall was born in 1498 or 1499, was educated at King's College, Cambridge, studied law at Gray's Inn and was at one time a Member of Parliament. In 1542 he published a history of the Wars of the Roses and the accession of the Tudor dynasty, under the impressive title:

The Union of the two noble and illustre families of Lancastre & Yorke, beeyng long in continual discension for the croune of this noble realme, with all the actes done in bothe the tymes of the princes bothe of the one linage and of the other, beginnyng at the tyme of Kyng Henry the Fowerth, the first aucthor of this deuision, and so successuiuely proceadyng to the reigne of the high and prudent prince Kyng Henry the Eight, the undubitate flower and very heire of both the sayd linages.

The whole tone of the title indicates the scope of the book, and if that were not enough, the introduction draws attention, in its very first sentence, to the miseries caused by internal warfare in so many European countries. Hall was born at a time when England was still recovering from years of such dissension; throughout his childhood and formative years the instinctive feeling of Englishmen was that a repetition of it must be avoided at all costs, and that, in sum, is the theme of his history. The very chapter-headings are adroitly pressed into service and made to underline his points, as may be seen when one goes through their titles in succession, thus:

An introduccion into the deuision of the two houses of Lancastre and Yorke.

i. The unquiet tyme of kyng Hēry the Fowerth
ii. The victorious actes of kyng Henry the v.
iii. The troubleous season of kyng Henry the vi
iiii. The prosperous reigne of kyng Edward the iiij.
v. The pitiful life of kyng Edward the v.
vi. The tragicall doynges of kyng Richard the iij.
vii. The polityke gouernaunce of kyng Henry the vij.
viii. The triumphant reigne of king Henry the viij.

That list suggests that the book has a story to tell. Moreover, the author's plea for internal peace had become relevant again some ten years before Shakespeare's birth. Mary Tudor's accession, the Spanish marriage, Wyatt's rebellion, the nine-days' reign of the ill-fated Jane Grey, and the burning of the Protestant martyrs had combined to show men in England how real the danger was, and how near any man or woman, whether a simple

London tradesman or Elizabeth, the queen's own sister and heir, might come to the fires of Smithfield or the scaffold and the axe on Tower Green. The allegorical tableaux at Elizabeth's accession had hailed her as the deliverer, the peace-bringer, the descendant of that Henry Tudor whose victory at Bosworth Field had put an end to the earlier years of civil strife and brought England back to prosperity. Hall's book might be over 20 years old by the time Shakespeare was born, but its theme was very far from being out of date, and had indeed acquired a new and terrible topicality, and it was from this that Shakespeare would get his first impressions of real English history, and with them some of his most durable ideas about it.

It is not mere coincidence that with the exception of *King John*—admittedly a revision of an old play by somebody else—Shakespeare's cycle of Histories follows Hall's chapter-list almost exactly, starting, as Hall does in his Introduction, with the downfall of Richard II and the first intrusion of the house of Lancaster and ending with the 'Triumphant Reign of King Henry VIII' and the christening of Elizabeth herself. The Prosperous Reign of King Edward IV and the Politic Governance of King Henry VII are, it is true, merely taken for granted, but neither prosperous reigns nor politic government are necessarily 'good theatre', and what is more important—the function of each as a bringer of peace and prosperity—is given full emphasis in the closing couplets of *Henry VI* and *Richard III* respectively. Even in the 'odd man out' we see the influence of Hall's teaching, for though Hall did not tell the story of the early Plantagenets, his theme, and Shakespeare's, is splendidly epitomized in the Bastard's last speech at the end of *King John*. Shakespeare and Hall, in fact, had each grown up in the years of recovery after a period of civil strife, and it is not surprising that the playwright found it possible, and desirable, to dramatize the narrative and philosophy of the historian.

Looked at in this way, the order of composition makes unexpected sense. The most sensational instance of Hall's theme is the loss of the English lands in France while the nobles are quarrelling at home during the minority of Henry VI, and the young dramatist quite reasonably begins with that. For all we know, he may have meant to leave matters there, but with its variety of combats, its artillery effects and a fine part for Talbot, the play was highly successful and made money. The natural thing, then, would be to go on, and this time we have rather more form than before. Instead of a series of mixed sensation-scenes, good in themselves but almost independent of each other, the remaining Henry VI plays show the working-out of the basic idea. The jealousy of the nobles, each playing for his own hand, leads to the bloodshed and massacre consequent on Jack Cade's revolt, and to the tragic, unnamed figures on the battlefield of Towton, one of whom has unwittingly killed his own father, the other his son, while the unhappy king Henry, powerless to help or hinder, is soon hurried away in his turn to imprisonment and death. Edward of York, triumphant in prosperity in the closing scene, is shown sick and worn out in the next play, trying to reconcile the newest Court dissensions and mourning the death of his brother Clarence, killed on his own too-hasty command. By the end of *Richard III* there have been several more executions and a murder, a pitched battle on English soil and the return of peace with the accession of a new dynasty.

After that, it would hardly be wise to take the story further, and to handle the reign of Henry VIII, however triumphant, with Henry's daughter on the throne of England and reasonably well disposed to the Chamberlain's Men, with whom Shakespeare was now acting and for whom he was writing. The theme, however, was not played out, and it was quite legitimate, and reasonably safe, to turn to the beginning of the book and dramatize the Introduction by writing a play about Richard II. A certain amount of care was naturally necessary—when the play was published as an independent quarto the scene of the king's formal deposition was tactfully omitted while Elizabeth was still alive—but it gave good opportunities for pageantry and still more for pathos. The main idea comes from Hall, but we can see that Shakespeare naturally looked up the subject in such other chronicles as he could lay his hands on. A remark about the withering of the bay-trees in Wales, for instance, indicates that he must have consulted the 1587 edition of Holinshed, since it is not to be found in the other chronicles. Richard's delivery of an actual crown to Henry of Bolingbroke is described in Hall but not in Holinshed, his surrender of his royal ring to the duke of York, and his formal release of his subjects from their allegiance, are in Holinshed but not in Hall. Shakespeare's treatment of the deposition-scene shows an adroit use of both authorities, and in his account of the conspiracy of York's son against the newly-crowned Henry—the event that precipitates Richard's murder in the interests of national security—he follows Hall implicitly, while Holinshed, though he repeats Hall's narrative, regards it with suspicion and appears to prefer a different account, given by Thomas Walsingham.

So it goes on. The general effect is always the same—the dramatist giving the story as he had learnt it originally, but putting in such trimmings and corroborative detail as he can pick up from later authorities. In *Henry V*, for instance, the opening is pure Hall, with its expressive account of the Church's reaction to a proposal to confiscate some of its property, and its uncomplimentary character-sketch of the archbishop of Canterbury. Holinshed gives a brief summary of the archbishop's exhortation to the king about his right to the French crown; Hall and Shakespeare give the whole speech in almost identical words.

When he gets to the reign of Henry VIII, Hall is particularly interesting and valuable, because he himself saw and heard many of the events and speeches he describes. Speaking of the arrival of Francis I of France with his retinue at the Field of Cloth-of-Gold, he says expressly, 'I then perceived the habiliment royal of the French king', and goes on to describe it in some detail. Likewise, his account of the conversation of the two cardinal-legates with the unhappy queen Katherine some years later contains the statement that 'these words were spoken in French, and written by cardinal Campeius' secretary, which was present, and by me translated as near as I could'. When he was not himself an eye-witness, Hall got his material for this reign as often as possible from those who were.

A few pages after this, in the 21st year of the king's reign, comes a sentence worthy of Tacitus for the way in which it combines extreme simplicity of style with extraordinary vision and significance. 'The King, which all the twenty years past had been ruled by others, and in especial by the Cardinal of York, began now to be a ruler and a king.' Here is the culmination of the whole story, the justification of the book's long and elaborate title, and here, if we consider it a little, is the theme of Shakespeare's play. Actors, actresses and producers have done so much with the rhetoric of Wolsey, the pathos of Katharine and the splendid pageantry of the cardinal's banquet and the coronation of Anne Boleyn that they have concentrated all their efforts, and the audience's interest, on those two 'mighty opposites', Queen of England and Prince of the Church, and Henry himself has been almost ignored.

This could hardly have been what Shakespeare intended, as it upsets the balance of the play completely, and it is obviously not what Hall intended, as when his book was first published, Henry was still alive and terrible. Whatever one felt about him, one could not—*dared* not—ignore him. Hall died in the same year as Henry, and it was his publisher Richard Grafton who carried the story on, in later editions, into the reign of Edward VI. To Hall, who never lived to see the troubles into which the country fell in that reign and the next, the emancipation of Henry was the happy ending to the long, unhappy tale that had begun with the fall of Richard Plantagenet nearly 150 years before.

With the death of Elizabeth, and the peaceable succession of another dynasty, it was possible for Shakespeare at last to round off the cycle of the Histories as Hall had done, making his 'happy ending' the christening of the infant Elizabeth, and contriving to incorporate in it a complimentary reference to king James. When we look at the text to see how he does it, we find episode after episode transferred to the stage from Hall's narrative, and with that illuminating sentence of Hall's to guide us we can see much more clearly what they are doing there, and how they contribute to the development of the play.

First of all, the Prologue makes it clear to the spectators that what they are going to see is a story not only tragic but historically true, and a clear demonstration of the rapidity with which 'mightiness meets misery'. Indeed, it appears from a contemporary letter that the title of the play when first produced was *All is True*. It is Shakespeare's way of indicating that the history of real people can be as exciting and moving as any romantic invention.

The opening conversation between the dukes of Norfolk and Buckingham is one of many that occur throughout the play and serve a double purpose. Like so many of Shakespeare's messenger-speeches, they are contrived to tell the spectators not only what the speaker wants his interlocutor to know about this or that, but what the author wants the audience to know about the giver of the news and its recipient. Norfolk's account of the Field of Cloth-of-Gold is splendid enough, but when he mentions that the organizer was 'the right reverend Cardinal of York', Buckingham breaks out in furious indignation, like one of the quarrelling nobles of the Henry VI plays. In a few lines he is revealed as powerful, arrogant and indiscreet to the point of foolhardiness. Even as Norfolk tries to check him, Shakespeare makes use of an effect which has served him well in the past in the first scene of *Hamlet*, when the speakers are cut short, in the height of their discussion, by the appearance of an ominous figure which passes across the stage with no word to them, and strikes them to a momentary silence. This time, instead of a ghost in armour, it is a little procession—some of the Guard, a man bearing the square purse, like a flat, stiff cushion, that is supposed to hold the Great Seal, and two secretaries with papers, attending the red-robed figure of the great cardinal on his way to the king. He has no word for the nobles as he goes by them; he and Buckingham exchange looks of disdain, and as he goes on his way he beckons one of his secretaries, asks him a couple of questions and goes out with a sinister remark that Buckingham is meant to overhear.

He does overhear it, and his reaction when the cardinal is out of earshot is to burst into still more intemperate railing and denunciation, accusing Wolsey of something very like treason.

Even as he swears he can make good his accusations, officers enter with a guard, and Buckingham and his son-in-law are arrested by a sergeant-at-arms. The news brings him up short; there is no railing, no passionate protest. The names of certain others are mentioned as having warrants out against them, and though as yet they may have no clear meaning for the audience, they obviously mean something to Buckingham, for he takes leave of Norfolk quietly and without hope, as a man already condemned to die.

Henry VIII in youth and age. The two portraits, from contemporary medals illustrated by John Evelyn, very well suit the different aspects of Shakespeare's Henry, and the author gives him ample time to change from the one make-up to the other as the play goes on.

In a single scene, the author has presented us in succession with vivid description of splendour, bold character-drawing, sudden heightening of the tension and an abrupt, stunning shock, leaving us in expectation of more ominous things to come. We have got to know Buckingham so well that it is hard to believe he has only two appearances in the play, but it is so, and and one of them is already over.

The entry of the king in the next scene, 'leaning on the cardinal's shoulder' as the stage direction has it, creates a triple effect at once, before he has uttered a word. It shows Henry in a characteristic, traditional attitude, as typical of him, in people's minds, as the snort of 'Ha!' with which the dramatist later makes such effective play. We must not think of Henry as the vast, gouty figure of the later Holbein portraits, needing a man's shoulder to lean on as he moves slowly and agonizingly to his throne. This is the pre-Holbein Henry, still young, athletic and reputed to be the handsomest man in Europe, the Henry who could write songs like 'The hunt is up' and 'Pastime with good company', and who could walk freely and informally with an arm flung across the shoulders of a familiar friend. The gesture shows that king and minister are on easy, confidential terms, and suggests that Wolsey's designs against Buckingham have already gone a stage further, as the duke's enemy has very clearly got the ear of the king.

If king Henry is played as a likeable character from the start, we can see the play taking shape. This Hal, like another Hal over 100 years before, is seen in danger of being misled and corrupted because he has bestowed his trust unworthily. More recent plays had shown how Laertes had been deceived, corrupted and destroyed by Claudius of Denmark, Roderigo by Iago, and—very nearly, though he just escaped it—Count Bertram by Parolles. Hall disliked prelates in general, and Wolsey in particular, and though his personal feelings are toned down by Holinshed when incorporating extracts from him in his own chronicle, Shakespeare seems to get his general ideas, as usual, from the earlier historian. Wolsey has warned the king of a dangerous conspiracy that has just been brought to light, and Buckingham's surveyor is on the point of being produced for questioning, when the tension is again unexpectedly suspended. The episode of the queen's entry at this point is not taken from any of the chroniclers, but is Shakespeare's own contribution to the drama, so the long and detailed stage direction introducing it is worth a little serious consideration. Usually, when there are elaborate directions in this play, they are details of processions and ceremonies described by Hall, but here we have nothing of that sort. It is in because the author considered it important that the entry should be made at that point and in that way. He wanted to be sure that not only the words but the stage business made their contribution to the drama. Quite possibly, in his retirement at Stratford, he knew that he would not be able to get up to London for rehearsals, and found it all the more important, therefore, to make his meaning plain by adding these individual points of production.

What exactly are they, and what is their effect? First, the shock of interruption, just as the examination is going to start, by a 'noyse within crying roome for the Queene'. Next moment she is there, with the dukes of Norfolk and Suffolk in attendance. Her affectionate welcome by the king, and his readiness to grant her suit before she can name it, are important not only because they show the mutual love and happiness of Henry and Katharine, but because we see an alliance that may after all be effective against the designs of Wolsey, and for a few moments it appears that it will be. The king flares up on hearing her story of taxation levied in his name and without his knowledge, and asks the cardinal some awkward and peremptory questions before ordering him to send out letters countermanding the tax and granting full pardon to those who have refused to pay. This episode, and Wolsey's ingenuity in taking credit for the remission of the tax, are taken from Hall's account of a later year, but are adroitly put in here by way of suggesting tension between the cardinal and the queen.

When Buckingham's surveyor is brought in to inform against his master, it needs no special pleading by the cardinal to stir the king to anger. The duke's own sayings and doings, as reported by his discharged officer, are enough for that, and though the queen is able, by a quiet interjection, slightly to discredit the informer, there is so much evidence, backed by names, dates and places, that the charge is obviously too grave to be set aside. Even if Buckingham has done no specific act of treason, he has indulged in too much wishful thinking, and unwise talking, about the king's death and his own possibilities of advancement, and the king sends him summarily to stand trial by his peers. The Wars of the Roses are not to break out again, as they may do if a rebellious subject is allowed to grow too great or live too long. After all, it was for taking just that sort of resentment one stage further that the earl of Essex had come in his turn to trial and execution some 12 years before the play was put on at the Globe, and that Ralegh, at the very time of the production, was living in the Tower under suspended sentence of death.

The conversation that opens the next scene seems to have little meaning for the average actor, producer or general reader. It is another piece of what one may call 'just Shakespeare', unless one follows the 19th-century critics who decided that it must be by somebody else. Lord Sands and the Lord Chamberlain are commenting on the extravagant French fashions brought back by a good many English courtiers from the Field of Cloth-of-Gold, and Sir Thomas Lovell comes in to tell them that these new tricks of costume and behaviour have just been put down by proclamation. On the face of it, the little episode has no effect on the action, so it is not immediately clear why Shakespeare put it in at all, and many may claim that it might be omitted without loss.

Once again, Hall provides the explanation. In his narrative it comes rather earlier, before the Field of Cloth-of-Gold, not after it, and some of the young men are named as having been indulged at the French court after the campaign of Tournai. Both Holinshed and Stow thought it worth incorporating in their own works, and it is clear that all these chroniclers, and Shakespeare after them, considered it important. So it is, in view of the light it throws on Henry's character, especially if we remember that the Henry of this part of the play is young, and might have been expected to share these extravagances rather than to discourage them. Once again we have a parallel with that other Hal who

> hath intent his wonted followers
> Shall all be very well provided for,
> But all are banished, till their conversation
> Appear more wise and modest to the world.

The young king, in fact, is developing, and showing a sense of responsibility.

The episode of Henry's arrival in disguise at the cardinal's banquet is not related by Hall, but by George Cavendish, Wolsey's gentleman-usher, in a biography not then in print but cited both by Holinshed and Stow. For dramatic purposes, Shakespeare makes it the occasion of Henry's first meeting with Anne Bullen—and, incidentally, the only scene in the play in which the two appear together. Henry speaks some half a dozen lines to her in all, while she has nothing to say in answer, yet from this meeting, under the disapproving eyes of Wolsey, springs a passion that is ultimately to ruin the cardinal and queen Katharine alike.

The account of Buckingham's trial is taken straight from Hall —who quite possibly saw it, as he was a law student at Gray's Inn at the time—as is the scene in which the condemned man passes, with the edge of the axe towards him, to the barge which is to take him one stage further towards his death. Critics have complained that Shakespeare has not made it sufficiently clear whether or not we are expected to sympathize with Buckingham, but in matters of history in general, and in this play in particular, it is his practice to marshal as much evidence as he can on both sides of a question, put it into the mouths of one character or another, and leave the audience to consider that evidence and draw their own conclusions. The purpose of a trial at law is to discover the truth and do justice, and the speeches of the First Gentleman, if properly spoken, should convey to the Second Gentleman, and to us who hear them, the speaker's reluctant conviction that the truth *has* been discovered and that, on the evidence, justice has been done.

In the matter of the validity of the king's marriage, Shakespeare declines to do our thinking for us. As before, he shows us the various schools of thought in the matter, and leaves it at that. He is not creating characters, he is depicting them by trying to reproduce, as far as possible, the various things they are known to have done and said, and it has been alleged on this account that his faculties were weakening, and that he was no longer capable of doing more. The charge, however, seems unjustifiable. The play deals with comparatively recent events, and there is little room for guesswork, even the inspired guesswork that is born of Shakespeare's imagination, when he has such a wealth of recorded fact to work from. In the matter of the proposed divorce he follows Hall and the other chroniclers by alluding to an early rumour promulgated in 1527 and sharply contradicted by the king, then to its renewal on the arrival of Campeius and the popular idea that Wolsey was at the back of it, out of enmity to Katharine's nephew the Emperor and desire to make an alliance with France.

This is Norfolk's view, while the breezy and ribald Suffolk (whose own matrimonial arrangements and rearrangements were notorious in their day) maintains that the king's conscience 'has crept too near another lady', but Shakespeare makes no attempt, either in this scene or in any other, to show that either of them is right in his assumption. What we do find in their conversation is the wish that Henry could learn to recognize the cardinal's influence and capacity for intrigue. We even see them preparing to warn him themselves, but he is nervous and irritable, and they get short shrift. Next moment he is eagerly welcoming Wolsey's introduction of Campeius, newly come from Rome to judge the case jointly with Wolsey as representatives of the Pope. Hall makes a point of the king's insistence that the queen should have the best lawyers and divines obtainable to advise her and put her case before the legates, and of his reluctant decision to avoid further intimacy with her until the matter could be cleared up one way or the other, and Shakespeare duly echoes him in this scene, but without Hall to guide us we are apt to misinterpret Henry's expression of the latter resolve. At least one well-known producer in living memory took it that Henry had already set his mind on a permanent divorce, and that his last lines in the scene should be over-played as a piece of comic hypocrisy, but comparison of the scene with the source-material does not support that interpretation. It is part of the facile but regrettable assumption that this is a bad play, only made tolerable by larding it with pageantry and cheap laughs and cutting out half the end.

Looked at from a more modern standpoint, the situation seems coherent, logical and very human. A husband who has been comfortably married for 20 years, but now has cause to fear that he is not legally married at all, is not unlikely, when dutifully keeping apart from his own wife, to develop an interest in another woman, particularly if she is young, attractive and a good listener. A natural reaction is to take every opportunity of praising the first wife while at the same time deploring the fact that apparently she has not, and never can have, the right to such a title. It is not conscious hypocrisy, merely an anxiety to avoid all unpleasantness and persuade himself that he has acted honourably and generously, while taking care at the same time to get what he wants. Once again let it be remembered that the Henry of the play is nearer to the young, clean-shaven Henry of the beginning of the reign than the gross figure, compounded apparently of Falstaff and Captain Macheath, whom we associate with the end of it.

Wolsey's influence over the king is hinted at, in this scene, in another way. Henry calls for Gardiner, his new secretary, mentioning that he finds him 'a fit fellow', and in two low-toned sentences between Wolsey and the newcomer we learn that the latter has been the cardinal's man and owes to him his present advancement. Indeed, Campeius does more than hint that Wolsey created the vacancy by getting the last secretary continually sent abroad on unnecessary embassies to keep him out of the way. If not exactly a spy, Gardiner is at least a useful instrument of Wolsey's policy, to be kept close about the king.

Another viewpoint is given us in the next scene, where a matter-of-fact old court lady sees quite clearly how matters are going and has no hesitation in saying so, especially when the Lord Chamberlain brings the news that the king has accorded Anne the title of Marchioness of Pembroke and an income of £1000 a year. This elevation really happened three years later, but once again Shakespeare has taken a slight liberty with the order of events and put in the story where it will be of most use in the development of the play.

Now comes rather a complicated piece of setting for an open Elizabethan stage. The entry of a long and elaborate procession, preceded by a fanfare of trumpets, would command the attention

A court sitting 'in manner of a Consistory' in a small boarded enclosure with the clerks' table in the centre and guards around the barriers.

of the audience and, as it came in at one of the side doors and passed along the front of the stage, would mask the activities of the scene-shifters in the middle. The two raised chairs for the cardinal-legates (draped and cushioned in cloth-of-gold, if the production was following Hall's description) could have been set ready in position on the inner stage, to be revealed by the drawing back of the central curtains, but benches for counsel and a central table for the clerks would have to be brought on and draped, and probably some light portable barriers to surround them, so that the members of the court could take their places 'in manner of a consistory'. Outside this, on the judges' right, would be set the king's chair, three steps higher than that of the judges and backed by a cloth of estate hung on the stage wall, while on the opposite side of the court was a chair for the queen to sit behind her counsellors.

The formality of the entry and the setting gives added force to the queen's spontaneous appeal when her name is called. In leaving her place, and going right round the court to kneel at her husband's feet, she is doing something highly irregular and quite unexpected, and the whole stage picture helps to emphasize the fact. How irregular it was, we can see from the fact that Hall does not mention it. With some equivocation he decides, presumably, that an unofficial, personal plea does not count, and so writes that 'the Quene departed without any thyng saiyng'. King Henry, when Hall's book appeared, had just had his fifth wife, Katharine Howard, beheaded for infidelity, so it would obviously be advisable to avoid reference to the emotional side of his married life. Cavendish never published his own account at all, though both Holinshed and Stow printed extracts from it in their own chronicles when Henry was safely dead.

Altogether, the queen makes a better show than the cardinals in this scene, and the king frankly admires her for it, and says so. His speech in explanation of his own position comes partly from Cavendish, partly from an earlier speech, recorded by Hall 'as nere as my witte could beare away', but by the end of the scene he is muttering at 'this dilatory sloth and tricks of Rome', and impatient for the counsel of Cranmer. His last 'Break up the court. I say, set on!' is an excellent theatrical device, as it gives the attendants every excuse for haste in clearing the chairs and tables out of the way while the procession is re-forming and going out.

Now, almost in the exact middle of the play, comes the turning-point and what may be called the king's emancipation. Cranmer has brought home the considered opinions of the principal universities of Europe, who have declared the king's marriage to be void, whereupon Henry has secretly married Anne Bullen. In addition, he has come across a letter from Wolsey urging the Pope to delay his decision of the case yet further because of the king's infatuation for Anne, and to crown all, in mistake for some official papers the cardinal has sent him the inventory of his own vast possessions. When the two men meet, Henry speaks courteously but with a new, quiet strength, and with a wealth of *double entendre* that the attendant nobles understand, though the cardinal does not, till the king in sudden sternness gives him the documents again and abruptly takes his leave. In Hall's expressive phrase, he has 'begun now to be a ruler and a king'.

The rest of the act is Wolsey's, and the author allows him to make the most of it. He has entered full of pride and power, arrogantly arranging in his mind the king's next marriage, to a princess of France, and deciding that Anne and Cranmer must be suppressed. It is with a sense of relief that we see his plans discovered and frustrated, and though he is soon figuring out a way to avoid the consequences of one revelation, he is appalled and checkmated by the other, and the result is complete collapse.

On the empty stage of the Globe there need be little or nothing to establish rigid continuity of time or place. It would be some days later, and at his great palace of Whitehall, that the nobles come to demand the surrender of the Great Seal, and to taunt him with his fall from favour. He faces them with courage, dignity and self-restraint, and we find ourselves even admiring him for his bearing in adversity. Then, in his famous scene with Cromwell, he passes from philosophy to plain simplicity and humility. As far as wordly power and possessions go, he has had everything, and has lost everything, and is unexpectedly at peace.

In more than one respect he shows a resemblance, at this stage, to his great enemy Buckingham. Each one is the better, and the happier, for the realization that to all intents and purposes he has left the world behind, each one speaks of the king with affection and generosity, and each looks forward humbly yet hopefully to the mercy of heaven.

During all this long scene the king is off the stage, and the whole of the next act is played without him. The rise of queen Anne is both described and depicted for us in the first scene by the passing of the coronation procession across the stage and by the comments of our old friends the First and Second Gentlemen, probably leaning over the rail of the upper gallery and pointing out individual figures below. The combination of speech and stage-direction is interesting and significant. Shakespeare was trying to make this play a record, as far as possible, of historical fact rather than a piece of theatrical invention. Writing at Stratford, out of close touch with the theatre management, he could hardly tell what resources the theatre would have by the time of the production, or how many supernumeraries it would be prepared to pay, but the stage direction, judiciously abridged from Hall (who presumably saw the ceremony), shows what he wanted, while the lines of the two Gentlemen indicate what he considered the absolute minimum for the proper presentation of the play.

By way of contrast we are then shown how Katharine, ill and neglected at Kimbolton, hears the news of Wolsey's last illness and death. Her relentless summary of his character is really Hall's, but Griffith, her gentleman-usher, begs leave to recall his good points in their turn. He does so, in terms which Shakespeare got from Holinshed, who had got them from a book written by Edmund Campion the Jesuit, but they are now transfigured with the true Shakespearean music, and move the injured queen to think of him more kindly and speak of their ancient antagonism as a thing of the past.

Her first thought, however, is one of appreciation and

gratitude for 'such an honest chronicler as Griffith', before she too, like Buckingham and Wolsey, finds herself drifting free from the anxieties of this world in her blissful contemplation of the next. Perhaps we may read a deeper meaning into Griffith's speech, and her acknowledgement of it. Throughout the play, as we have seen, Shakespeare has tried to be scrupulously fair to history, and to all the characters concerned, by keeping as close as possible to such evidence as he can get. Some commentators have censured the play and its author because it is not 'true tragedy', but have not always realized that this is deliberate, because the author was trying to present true history, which is a very different thing. The actual events of life do not always arrange themselves in well-constructed dramatic form, and the scene may remind us that the 'honest chronicler' is not undeserving of our praise.

Certain liberties have to be taken now and then, notably in the matter of time. The chronology of the last act is somewhat elastic, as Gardiner's arraignment of Cranmer did not coincide with Elizabeth's birth but took place a good many years after. The story, however, is so good, and so dramatic, that one can understand Shakespeare's decision to make use of it, particularly as it is a clear illustration of Henry's determination—and ability—to handle matters of state himself, instead of depending on his ministers for information and advice. It is not Hall, but Foxe, who tells of Henry's summoning Cranmer to the palace by night, warning him of the design against him and handing him the ring which he later produces so dramatically at the council-board. Much of the king's part in these scenes is taken almost word for word from the *Actes and Monuments of the Martyrs*. Foxe got his information from Cranmer's secretary Ralph Morice; Morice had had it from Cranmer, and Cranmer would have cause to remember clearly enough what the king said to him, and to the Council that tried to humiliate and imprison him. There is a great deal in the lines that has the authentic Tudor ring about it and suggests that we have something that really echoes the great Henry in a rage. And it is the Holbein Henry by this time. Quite possibly during his long absence throughout the fourth act, the actor (said to be John Lowin) was in the tiring-house altering his appearance and adding the right sort of beard to bring him into line with the crude woodcut in Holinshed and the memories of some who might be in the audience. Men who were in their mid-70s in 1613 would have been boys of nine or ten when Henry died.

So the play reaches its climax—the climax of Hall's story of the reign, and of the strife and ambition and bloodshed that had led up to it. The king of England enters 'frowning on them' and takes his seat, browbeats nobles and bishop alike and speaks out in favour of an honest man unjustly accused. That is what audiences want to see, and what the dramatist wants to show them. After that, there is no need for more except a brisk rude scene with a comic porter and his man, another procession, with 'everybody on for the end', and the final production and proclamation of the baby whom the spectators would remember as having been

> to the happiness of England
> An aged princess.

It may not be what some of Shakespeare's admirers would have chosen for his concluding play, but it is a fitting close, none the less, to the story of that turbulent century and a half in the history of England.

VIII

The Stage Picture

Public theatres in Shakespeare's time had not much in the way of scenery. There were hangings of tapestry or painted cloth, much as there would be in most London houses of any consequence, and we know there was a certain amount of stage furniture in the way of stools, thrones, arbours, statues and the like, which could be set in position or taken away as required, but there seems to have been little or nothing to serve as a specific, localized background against which the actors would play. Theatres did not provide it, audiences did not expect it, authors did not write for it, and in consequence everybody got on reasonably well without it. The main function of pictorial scenery is to provide a background. The characters in a play may depend, for their dramatic effectiveness, on their relation to their setting, whether they are in harmony with it, as in a play like *Quality Street*, or in revolt against it, as in the social dramas of Ibsen and his successors. Shakespeare and his contemporaries, in the absence of any such dumb indication of the setting, showed the characters from the outset in their relation to one another. The sentries challenging each other in the cold night at Elsinore, the Merchant of Venice admitting to his business colleagues that he is out of sorts, Richard II nervously questioning his uncle about an impending quarrel, all show us in the first moment something of their character and their feelings. We see *what* they are, we are not long in grasping *who* they are, and we have no immediate need to know just *where* they are. When it is time for us to know, somebody indicates it in conversation, but we do not have the location forced upon us at the outset if the author wants us to direct our attention to something else. The different scenes are not scenes of people in different places, but in different company, or the same company in different situations and under different strains. People, after all, are usually more important than places, especially if the dramatist takes deliberate care to make them so.

And how superlatively well Shakespeare does it! He does not strain the audience's credulity by alluding to things that are quite obviously not there; his verbal scene-painting is applied to objects or landscapes just off-stage. When an actor points to one side and says 'There stands the castle, by yon tuft of trees,' or 'Look, the unfolding star calls up the shepherd,' we do not need to see the trees or the castle or the sky paling with the first light of dawn. We see *him* seeing them, and that is enough, especially if we have nothing much else to occupy our attention. A painted stage-picture, if it is badly done, will irritate us; if it is well done, it will attract us, and in either event—in Shakespeare, at any rate—it will divert our full attention from the matter in hand, because the author has arranged to make his effects without this particular feature.

That does not mean that he makes no use of visual effects. There are indications again and again in the texts of the plays that he has a keen sense of the appearance of his characters, and now and then we can gain a little relevant information from outside sources. Descriptions of Elizabethan Venice tell us how it was the custom for a Venetian gentleman to appear in public gowned in black from neck to ankle, keeping his fine clothes for wear at home or on the mainland. Senators and Doctors wore gowns of scarlet, and Jews dressed in dark red with yellow caps. These gradations, well known to the inhabitants of a great mercantile city like London, would simplify the staging of *The Merchant of Venice*, which has so often caused a good deal of scene-shifting in the rapid alternation of the action between Venice and Belmont. Some managements, indeed, altered the order of the scenes, putting all the Venetian ones together and keeping Belmont and its lady waiting in the wings, as it were, till the elaborate Venetian 'set' could be struck, and give place to the hall of the caskets. Shakespeare, we may imagine, did things more simply. While Bassanio and his friends wore black gowns and little round hats, like portraits by Bellini, they were obviously at home in Venice; when they appeared a little later in doublet and hose it was clear that they must have crossed over to the mainland. The Prince of Morocco, when he comes to woo, is specified as 'a tawnie Moore all in white', and the Folio stage direction gives him 'three or four followers accordingly'—i.e., to match. That little group of 'outlanders', with their dark faces and white draperies, would give an expressive and ominous

Bassanio in Venice. Young Venetian noble in the long black gown customarily worn when appearing out of doors in Venice itself.

indication of the possible fate in store for Portia, and this unusually detailed direction suggests that that sense of hazard was just what the author intended.

The long dark gowns of Venice would perform another function likewise. Unobtrusively enough, they would predispose the audience to accept the possibility of Portia's effectively disguising herself in a similar dress and passing for a young man. By the time the idea comes to her, the play has been in progress for nearly three whole acts, and the spectators are quite used to the normal attire of Venetian gentlemen in their own city. Portia's disguise as the 'young doctor of Rome' would resemble it in cut, though its colour would be the doctorial scarlet, and she would not seem to be too obviously *en travesti*.

In the very first scene of *King Henry VI* another visual effect

Bassanio at Belmont, showing the doublet and 'Venetians', or close knee-breeches, worn at home or on the mainland.

may be intended. After the first messenger has interrupted the funeral of Henry V with the shocking news of the English losses in France, the duke of Bedford cries:

> Me they concern. Regent I am of France:
> Give me my steelèd coat, I'll fight for France.
> Away with these disgraceful wailing-robes;
> Wounds will I lend the French instead of eyes
> To weep their intermissive miseries.

It sounds very much as if the actor were meant to cast off, at this point, the great all-enveloping cloak and hood that were characteristic of Elizabethan funerals, and show himself either in armour or the velvet or leather under-dress habitually worn beneath it. His companions follow suit, and the scene goes on, with no further reference to the dead king or his funeral. Perhaps

Nobleman of Barbary, showing the probable appearance of the Prince of Morocco in *The Merchant of Venice*.

the coffin has been taken out with the mourning-cloaks, and to all intents and purposes the English nobles may be in some other place, a little later on, when they hear the reports of the second and third messengers, and make their dispositions accordingly.

And perhaps, once the coffin and mourning-cloaks are out of the way, one can accept subconsciously an alteration not only of place but of time. Those three messengers, with their different tidings and very different manner of conveying them, are not necessarily arriving hard on each other's heels. With no scenery or standing-properties to tie them down to one unaltering place or moment, one can see in these successive arrivals a more gradual process of disintegration across the Channel. There has been no sudden, all-embracing disaster, the English hold on France is weakening stage by stage, for reasons uncompromisingly given by the first messenger, and with that very fact begins the gradual downfall of the house of Lancaster, which is the theme of this and the two succeeding plays.

The same suggestion of progress in time occurs quite noticeably in two other plays. The most important instance is in the third act of *Othello*. At the beginning of it, Cassio comes to apologize for having made a drunken exhibition of himself the night before (he has not been to bed since, he tells Iago), and to ask Desdemona to intercede for him, showing us that this is their first full day in Cyprus. The action seems quite continuous, yet a little later on, Iago is arousing Othello's suspicions as if they had all been long enough in the island for Cassio to have enjoyed a secret intrigue with Desdemona. The incongruity sometimes jars on us when we read the text in a modern edition with localized settings for every scene, and also, though to a less extent, when we see the scene played in a realistic setting and know that nobody has had time to do anything in the way of misconduct, since we have seen them in one room in the castle, or terrace before the castle, we have watched their goings out and their comings in, and feel we can account for practically every minute of their time.

If, on the other hand, we have no reason to think of them in any localized setting, or against any specific background, we concentrate on the characters and their company, with less thought of where or when, and by the time Iago is gaining Othello's ear after the 'Excellent wretch!' outburst, we are ready to assume that their stay in Cyprus is by now some weeks old, and that Cassio has been all that time out of office, despite his remark at the beginning of the act. By the end of the scene, too, it seems even as if the loss of the handkerchief were an event in the not-very-recent past, even though it is only a matter of minutes since Othello dashed it out of Desdemona's hand. The stage picture, the visible grouping of the characters, changes with every entry or departure, and it is as if time were to move imperceptibly forward as each entry or exit inaugurated a new scene.

The other play where this is particularly noticeable is *Richard II*, where two scenes, of very different content, are habitually run into one at the beginning of the second act. As it is generally played, Northumberland enters to tell the king that John of Gaunt is dead, and without leaving the stage announces to Ross and Willoughby (who have conveniently stayed behind when everyone else went out with Richard and his queen) that Gaunt's son is coming back from exile, and they all hurry off to Yorkshire to join him in claiming his father's inheritance. This looks curiously sudden and improbable when played in the room from which we have just seen Gaunt carried out to die, and in the house that Richard has just claimed for himself and established as his headquarters. Ross and Willoughby have had nothing to say hitherto, and no reason to be there at all. At Burbage's Theatre in Moorfields the visual effect would have been that Gaunt's death-scene ended when the king *and everybody else* went off the stage. By the time Ross and Willoughby entered, and Northumberland came back to meet them with the words 'Well, lords, the duke of Lancaster is dead,' one would accept as a matter of course that the place was an unspecified Somewhere Else, and the time apparently Some Time Later, when the king's injustice and insolvency had become common knowledge and he was just setting sail for Ireland. Taken that way, the sight of three men discussing recent, secret and very welcome news takes on an extra quality of drama which we may safely assume that the author meant it to possess.

This absence of localized scenery must have made the combats and battle-scenes in some of the Histories a good deal easier to stage and more effective to watch, because when such a scene is played on a bare or nearly-bare Elizabethan stage, the action is concentrated, and the dramatic illusion sustained, more easily than in a fully-representational set. The minds and eyes of the spectators are concerned with the players alone, and there is no call to consider the parts of the stage that are not at the moment in use. In *III Henry VI*, for instance, a brisk combat of three or four a side, on an Elizabethan stage and before an Elizabethan audience, would sufficiently arrest the spectators' attention. There would be no stage-full of battling figures to confuse and distract the eye, and, conversely, no expanse of realistic but empty stage landscape to suggest that both armies were remarkably under-manned. The area that was not being fought over would be simply ignored, and as soon as the French had been driven out by the English, both parties could hurry round to the tiring-house and change for their encounter in the next scene. This time they would be serving-men in coloured surcoats—blue for the duke of Gloucester, tawny for the arrogant Cardinal Beaufort—brawling before the Tower gates until stopped and dispersed by the action of the Mayor.

But between these two scenes of military and civil skirmishing, Shakespeare has introduced a combat of a different kind. After the French have been beaten back from their attempt to relieve Orleans, the Dauphin and his colleagues are interrupted by the arrival of Joan the Maid, confident in her divine mission. The Dauphin challenges her to justify herself by a friendly bout, she accepts and is victorious, and without more ado he welcomes her as a champion and ally.

After thus giving his audience an infantry action, a hand-to-hand single combat and then a civilian brawl between two groups of serving-men, the author turns his attention to the possibilities of artillery. The death of Salisbury by a shot from one of the guns of Orleans is recorded in the chronicles of Hall, Grafton and Holinshed, and was obviously worth transferring to the stage if such a thing could be done. Here, again, the absence of definite, localizing scenery is an advantage. The master-gunner of Orelans simply comes on to the stage with his son, tells how he has laid a gun to command the English observation-post in the suburbs, and orders the boy to keep good watch while he himself is at the Governor's lodging. (The chronicles all say that he had gone off to his dinner, but this corroborative detail does not appear in the Folio text.) The gun is not seen, there is nothing to suggest that it is visible on the stage, and the words 'on the walls' in present-day texts are merely additions by a later editor. The gunner and his son have done enough, by their brief conversation, to show the audience what to expect when they see anyone appear on the upper stage, and as soon as the boy has gone—with a significant couple of lines when his father is out of earshot—we find the stage direction, 'Enter Salisbury and Talbot on the Turrets, with others.' They have not been there long before the boy reappears, carrying a burning linstock and presumably crossing the unlocalized lower stage. He has nothing to say, and needs nothing, as his appearance with the linstock is a clear enough indication of what he is going to do. The officers are visible above, looking through their barred window and pointing out suitable targets for the next assault or bombardment, and in a moment the sound of a gun is heard, and Salisbury and Sir Thomas Gargrave fall mortally wounded. There is a short thunderstorm for good measure, and with the next scene we are back at an ordinary straightforward battle. The trumpets sound an alarm, Talbot is seen driving the Dauphin before him, and then comes Joan in her turn, driving Englishmen before *her*. At last we see the French and English champions meeting for a hand-to-hand combat, probably something very different from the Maid's brief bout with the Dauphin on her first arrival in his camp. From the viewpoint of practical Elizabethan stagecraft, it is a bout between a leading actor—almost certainly an accomplished swordsman as a matter of course—and a promising boy-player of women's parts, who is allowed to show something of his form. Talbot is beaten down, Joan enters Orleans with her followers, the trumpets blow 'a short Alarum' and there is another skirmish, after which Talbot calls his men to retire. Finally there is the sound of a triumphant flourish, and Joan appears on the upper stage, with the Dauphin, his officers and their soldiers, so that there is no doubt that Orleans has been relieved. And all this variety of action—armed battle, civil brawl, friendly combat, hand-to-hand encounter in arms, alarums, excursions and sudden, devastating casualty from a heavy gun—has taken place in the first act alone. An Elizabethan audience, coming to the play for the first time, may well have paused for breath at this point and wondered if, and how, the author was going to keep up the excitement.

He does it without repeating his effects. Half a dozen lines at the beginning serve to set the scene; a French sergeant is seen mounting a guard on the upper stage, and as soon as he is out of the way the grumbling of a sentry shows that it is a dark, wet and chilly night. Talbot, Bedford and Burgundy enter below, set up scaling-ladders and mount to the attack, the French jump over the walls in their shirt-sleeves (a useful way of showing the audience which army is which), the Dauphin's colleagues 'enter severall wayes . . . halfe ready, and halfe unready' and finally Joan and the Dauphin themselves appear. They all fall to recrimination, each blaming one of the others for negligence, but when an English soldier approaches, shouting the name of Talbot, 'they flye, leaving their Clothes behind'. The soldier cheerfully makes off with the clothes, and after this touch of unexpected comedy, Bedford enters with Talbot and Burgundy, and commands a retreat to be sounded and the pursuit to be called off. It is quite clear that the town has been taken, and it is a tribute to the craftsmanship of the playwright that the effect has been so easily conveyed.

Sometimes a brief glimpse of a stage-property helps to set the *locale* in the audience's mind, or to show, without wasting time, what has been happening in the last few minutes. When the Yorkist princes break into the Parliament House at the opening of the Third Part of *King Henry VI*, the first line is 'I wonder how the king escaped our hands', and when Edward and Montague have shown their bloodstained swords and claimed to have killed the duke of Buckingham and the earl of Wiltshire, Richard of Gloucester startles them, and the audience, by throwing down before them the severed head of Somerset, with the words 'Speak thou for me, and tell them what I did.' A few lines later his words 'Thus do I hope to shake king Henry's head' suggest that he gets the property head out of sight by throwing it off-stage before it can lose its effect by showing itself too obviously a counterfeit from the tiring-house, and meanwhile the episode has served to illustrate in a little clearer detail the seriousness of the situation and the character of the future Richard III. Shakespeare does the same thing again, though with a lighter touch, in the third act of *King John*. The pompous, bullying duke of Austria has been driven to the brink of fury because the Bastard (a son of Richard Coeur-de-Lion) consistently refuses to take him seriously, and when war breaks out one might expect to see a terrific stage combat between them. But by this time Shakespeare knew a trick worth two of that. Consistent as ever, the Bastard comes on to the stage complaining that it is a very hot day, and our only indication of what he has just been doing is the realization that he is carrying Austria's head, which he puts down, presumably round the corner, with an adjuration to lie there until he gets his breath back. Next moment he has other things to attend to, so he never refers to it again. As a piece of masterly understatement, it has a kind of parallel in the technique of the late Sir George Robey, who would come on to the stage carrying a large ivory tusk in each hand, put them down in a corner out of sight, dust his hands against each other with the stern remark '*I'll* teach elephants to argue!' and go on to something else.

Possibly it is the element of formality that gives weight to certain types of Shakespearean stage direction. When Duncan has arrived at Macbeth's castle, we are told that 'a Sewer, and divers servants with dishes and service' should enter and pass over the stage before Macbeth comes in for his great soliloquy 'If it were done when 'tis done'. Very often this piece of business is left out, but when it is retained, the sight of a major-domo marshalling a little procession of servants carrying dishes across the stage instantly conveys the impression that a rather elaborate dinner is going on in the next room, and gives an air of urgency to the hurried colloquy between Macbeth and Lady Macbeth, since it is clear that in a moment they will have to get back to their guests. Likewise, later in the same play, the entry of Macbeth, Malcolm or the rebel thanes with 'drum and colours' tells us at once that there is an organized, disciplined body of troops immediately at hand. This effect is not, of course, restricted to Shakespearean performances alone. The late Sir John Martin-Harvey made good use of it in that rousing Civil War melodrama *The Breed of the Treshams*, where at the end of a highly exciting act the entry of an old Cavalier with drawn sword, attended only by a boy with a drum and a soldier with a military flag of the regular 17th-century type, gave a complete and satisfactory impression of the arrival of a relieving force in the nick of time.

This drum-and-colours technique occurs in a good many of the plays, always with the significance of organization and formality. An interesting variant of it, which must have made a striking stage-picture, is the triumphal entry of Ventidius in *Antony and Cleopatra*. We have just seen the three rulers of the Roman world being feasted by Sextus Pompeius on board his galley. Octavius Caesar has had more to drink than he really wanted, Antony is in high spirits and obviously far from sober, Lepidus has passed out completely and has been carried away by an attendant, and Sextus Pompeius is slightly tearful, with his 'O Antony—you have my father's house—but what—we are friends.' The Triumvirs stagger off to their boat, Enobarbus has found an old acquaintance on board and goes whooping below to make a night of it, and the stage is clear for a moment. Then, by way of sharp contrast, 'Enter Ventidius as it were in triumph, the dead body of Pacorus borne before him.' We have left the straits of Messina for the Syrian desert; while Antony is drinking and joking in Sicily, his lieutenant in the east has been doing the work, and gaining the victory, that Antony should have accomplished long ago. The armies of Rome are marching and fighting on the frontier while their rulers are revelling at home, and an extra bite is given to the contrast when we hear Ventidius declining to follow up his victory because it does not do for a subaltern to be too successful in the absence of his chief. As it is, he intends to report the matter in terms that will allow Antony to take the credit for it. 'On there, pass along,' he cries, and the armed men march away. Next moment we are back in Europe again, but with a fuller knowledge of Antony now that we have seen—not only heard, but *seen*—what he is neglecting, and what some of his loyal followers not unjustly think of him.

Another interesting piece of staging from the visual point of view is the banquet scene in *Macbeth*, which uses a combination of formal state and extreme informality to work up a dramatic effect. Macbeth at the outset says:

> Ourself will mingle with society
> And play the humble host.
> Our hostess keeps her state, but in best time
> We will require her welcome.

In other words, Lady Macbeth is enthroned, probably on the upper stage (the usual place, as Sir Thomas Roe has shown us, for theatrical royalty) while Macbeth remains below, able to move about the acting-area, to approach a side door and have a word with a murderer upon the threshold, and in due course, we may assume, to offer to sit in the central seat, left glaringly unoccupied by the absence of Banquo until the dead man's ghost arrives to claim it. This gives the leading actor space and freedom to let himself go, in the emotional passages, to the fullest extent, while Lady Macbeth, high in her 'state', tries by her words and bearing to calm him down as befits the dignity of the occasion. Turning again to Hall, we may see where Shakespeare almost certainly got the idea. Henry VIII, in the very first year of his reign, held a banquet for all the foreign ambassadors who were then at Court, and when all was ready, 'the Kyng leading the Quene, entred into the Chambre, then the Ladies, Ambassadours and other noble menne, folowed in ordre. The Kyng caused the Quene, to kepe the estate, and then satte the Ambassadours and Ladyes as they were Marshalled by the kyng, who would not sit, but walked from place to place, making chere to the Quene, and the straungers.' This enabled him to slip out and return in disguise in a few minutes' time, and Shakespeare must have remembered this piece of royal informality and turned it to good account in a very different context.

Sometimes we get a very different impression of a scene when we study the text and original stage directions instead of those imposed on us by 18th-century editors. The arrival of Mercutio and his party at Capulet's ball is arranged in the Quarto by the direction, 'They march about the stage, and serving-men come forth with napkins.' There is no need for anything visibly to represent the streets of Verona; when we see the masquers and torch-bearers marching round the stage we know where they are meant to be going, and when they are received by serving-men carrying napkins like waiters, it is obvious that they have got there.

Capulet and his kinsman, by the way, appear to be looking on from the upper stage, while the ladies sit below, in accordance with Renaissance custom, and some of them take part in the dance. Tybalt on the balcony recognizes Romeo's voice but does not address him directly and is frantic because he cannot get at him. Looking at Capulet's lines, one can see how the situation is worked up, as his speech develops into a rapid alternation of sharp reproofs to Tybalt at his elbow and loud exhortations to the servants and the company, to distract their attention from Tybalt's behaviour and avoid the risk of anything like a scene. Put him up on the balcony, with his quarrelsome nephew and his elderly cousin, and his position is effectively contrasted with, yet not masked by, the formal, graceful dance taking place on the main stage, and on that balcony, it seems reasonable to suppose, the author meant to put him. It is up there, too, that Juliet possibly lingers on her way to bed, as she and the Nurse watch the last guests going out of the hall and the servants clear away the seats and what is left of the refreshments. The stage is cleared, in the most natural way imaginable, for the requirements of the next scene.

A few scenes later comes a visual effect suggested by a stage direction but nullified by the gratuitous insertion of a scene-location. With all respect to the scholars and editors of the 18th century, there is absolutely nothing in the text to imply that the first appearance of Friar Lawrence is located in his cell. The stage direction ordains that he should enter 'with a basket', and that, to the Elizabethan mind, would suggest at once that he was meant to be out of doors, and going about his business. His opening words about the sunrise are those of someone who is just enjoying his first taste of the morning air, and it is not, perhaps, impermissible to suggest that in the course of his opening speech he may have gone down on his knees, with basket and weeding-fork, as if searching for simples among the roots of one of the pillars that supported the canopy over the central part of the stage. His lines about 'the infant rind of this weak flower' sound very like appropriate meditation over something he has just carefully uprooted, and if he is still on his knees, and Romeo enters behind him, it is quite natural that he does not immediately know who has wished him good-morrow.

The very opening of the play is spectacular enough, with its arguments, quarrels and the sudden scuffle of a street brawl, but this in itself is notable for the way in which it is adapted to create the maximum effect with the minimum of actual numbers. For one thing, the company would not have a very large number on its pay-roll; for another, too many figures in violent movement would only clutter the stage and confuse the situation. As it is, we have Sampson and Gregory (who have opened the play with a conversation on the lines made familiar to us by Messrs Morecambe and Wise) on the one side, and Abraham and Balthasar on the other. Then Benvolio draws his weapon only to strike down theirs, and straight upon his heels comes Tybalt, whom Gregory has already seen in the distance and counted on as a supporter. The four serving-men are out for an ordinary sword-and-buckler 'punch-up' in which nobody is likely to get very seriously hurt, rather after the manner of the Irishman who asked, 'Is this a private fight, or may anyone join in?' Benvolio is merely trying to stop the trouble before it really begins, but Tybalt is the most dangerous of them all. He is Benvolio's social equal, he has found Benvolio with his sword drawn first, among the serving-men, so he has a glorious excuse for killing him and saying that the other man began it. His fight with Benvolio is therefore something much more serious and dangerous than the cheerful quarrelling of the sword-and-buckler men.

Then comes the stage direction 'Enter three or four Citizens with clubs or partisans.' We know more about them from the

Prince's speech later on. They are 'Verona's ancient citizens', in other words, the elderly gentlemen who constitute the Watch and are responsible for keeping the peace. They would use the hafts of their weapons and belabour both sides indiscriminately, though keeping discreetly clear of the noblemen as long as they can. Old Montague and Capulet can do little more than shake their fists, because Montague's wife is hanging on to his sword-arm and Capulet has no sword at all. (He is described as being 'in his gown', most probably because he has to be wearing his banqueting-dress underneath it, as there is little time for him to change.) By this time we have five a side (counting the ladies) and the three or four Citizens into the bargain, which would be quite enough for the average Elizabethan stage, and as much as an audience can conveniently watch without getting quite confused. When the Prince comes in, with his train, one would imagine that the serving-men would stop practically at once, and the Citizens would still be trying to separate Tybalt and Benvolio, to whom, principally, the lines appear to be addressed. The Prince's presence, and the sight of a few of his guards in livery coats of some sort, helps to make it clear from the outset that there are at least three important families in Verona, not merely two.

Quite possibly he is meant to make his appearance on the upper stage, and leave the field below clear for the skirmishing, just as Capulet later on may have left it clear for the dancing. Something of the same sort seems likely to have been intended in the scene of the friendly bout, in *Troilus and Cressida*, between Hector and Ajax, the champions of the opposing armies. This is a social event as well as a sporting one, and it is made the occasion for Cressida's first appearance in the camp of the Greeks, like a young woman of fashion making her first appearance at a smart race-meeting and attracting a certain amount of attention by her behaviour. Ulysses draws his own conclusions from it—by no means flattering to Cressida and her type—and then the Trojans' trumpet announces the arrival of the visiting team. The combatants themselves do not speak; it is Aeneas, Hector's second, who asks whether they are to fight to the death or till they are parted by orders from the rulers of the lists, and is told that he and Diomed, who is acting as second to Ajax, can arrange these points to suit themselves.

It would seem that Agamemnon, Menelaus, Achilles and Patroclus are meant to have gone up into the gallery over the stage after the arrival and reception of Cressida. Ulysses' little scene with her, and with Nestor after her departure, gives them time to do it, and to be visible up there by the time the Trojans are announced, Nestor and Ulysses following at their leisure. The succeeding dialogue certainly suggests that by this time Agamemnon is surveying the lists from the equivalent of the Tilt-yard Gallery at Whitehall, and one can imagine Achilles leaning over the railing to make his disdainful remarks to Aeneas while they are waiting for Diomed to arrive. The unheard discussion between the two seconds gives Ulysses time to get to his place and answer Agamemnon's enquiry about Troilus, who is presumably standing among Hector's supporters on the far side. The Folio stage direction specifies the entry of 'all of Troy, Hector, Paris, Aeneas, Helenus and Attendants', but there is no conversation between their party and Agamemnon's—not surprising, with Paris in the one and Menelaus in the other—and they may have done no more than pass across the stage and be presumed to be watching from the other end of the lists.

Then the trumpets sound an alarum, and the fight begins. After all this elaborate build-up, and its integration with the action and emotions of the play—not to mention its importance in the Homeric original—it *has* to be a good one, and the author has arranged his cast accordingly. As in the first play of all, his leading man can be trusted to fight well in addition to acting well, and his adversary must be a skilled fighter likewise, but that is practically all he need be. Shakespeare has taken care to present Ajax as a fine warrior but a fantastically stupid man—that is what makes him such an excellent 'feed' to Thersites—and it is quite safe, accordingly, to entrust the part to anyone who is a really good swordsman, even if he is a fantastically stupid actor. The fight is cheered on by exhortations from the oldest spectator on the one side and the youngest on the other, and then the trumpets give the signal to stop, and the seconds intervene and part the combatants. Ajax is quite ready to go on again, but Hector laughingly reminds him of their cousinship, and is content to let the matter end in 'embracement', taking the opportunity to compliment his adversary on his muscles as he does so.

This has given time for Agamemnon and his party to come down from their grand-stand and meet Hector on the ground, and the scene takes its course without any suggestion that we are still in the middle of the lists. The locale has moved unobtrusively to some unspecified part of the camp.

The conventional stage-picture at the end of *Antony and Cleopatra*, with Cleopatra sitting dead on her throne, is said to have been inspired by the performance of Janet Achurch in the part at Manchester, but the credit for it may rather be claimed for John Dryden, whose Cleopatra, in *All for Love*, is made to kill herself quite shortly after Antony, and the two dead lovers are clearly meant to be on thrones, as they are said to

> sit in state together
> As they were giving laws to half mankind.

Shakespeare's Cleopatra, on the contrary, is imagined to be lying on a bed. Charmian pretends that she is asleep when the Guard comes hurrying in, and Caesar himself makes the same comparison when he stands beside the bed that has become her bier. It looks as if Shakespeare wanted the audience to go home thinking of the great lover, rather than the great queen, and Caesar's lines bear out the same basic idea. To him there is no suggestion of giving laws to half mankind; what he thinks is that

> she looks like sleep,
> As she would catch another Antony
> In her strong toil of grace.

At this moment, perhaps for the first time, he sees what it was that irresistibly beckoned Antony away from his loyalty to Caesar and to Rome.

Evidence of the popularity of Shakespeare's play is provided by Fletcher in his Prologue to *The False One*, which deals with Julius Caesar's visit to Egypt in Cleopatra's girlhood. He says categorically that there is nothing wrong in writing about a historical character already treated by someone else, so long as one avoids direct plagiarism, that Caesar's 'amorous heats' are something very different from his death in the Capitol, and as for Cleopatra, the players

> treat not of what boldness she did die
> Nor of her fatal love for Antony.

The whole Prologue is worth comparing with the corresponding section of Shaw's Preface to *Caesar and Cleopatra* (where, in his own characteristic way, he says very much the same thing) and appears to have escaped the notice of those scholars who maintain that *Antony and Cleopatra* was never produced in its author's lifetime, but the general impression it gives is that the play, and *Julius Caesar*, were sufficiently well established in common knowledge for some such disclaimer to be necessary if another play about the principal characters were to get a hearing. Indeed, the blunt and disrespectful Enobarbus of *Antony and Cleopatra* has evidently achieved reincarnation, in due course, in Fletcher's Scaeva, possibly Dryden's Ventidius and, surprisingly but quite unquestionably, Shaw's Rufio. One would not normally suspect Shaw of flattering Shakespeare, but are we not told, after all, that imitation is the sincerest flattery?

That final sight of the apparently-sleeping queen, in her royal ornaments, carried slowly from the stage on the shoulders of her enemies is something that must have impressed itself on a good many minds, including Dryden's. We can well imagine his anxiety to avoid at all costs anything that could be construed as an imitation of the earlier play's effects. By 1678, the date of *All for Love*, the theatre had a curtain to be lowered, and it was possible to end the tragedy with the tableau of those two lovers sitting upright in their chairs, like statues of the gods, and there is something ironic in the thought that this effect, which may have been introduced as a deliberate contrast to the Shakespearean ending, has become the more or less unquestioned practice of producers with the Shakespearean Cleopatras of today.

IX

Combats, and their Problems

Elizabethan audiences knew a good deal about fights, and were qualified to be critical. Quite apart from the periodical 'musters', and periods of brief but intensive military training that took place at Mile End and elsewhere, there was the traditional sword-and-buckler play with which the London apprentices exercised themselves of a summer evening before a festival like May Day or Midsummer Day. For those who preferred looking on to taking part, there were occasional displays or prize-fights with blunt (but not very blunt) weapons, giving the spectators a chance to do a certain amount of betting and see a certain amount of bloodshed, with hard knocks but little or no hard feeling, and for those who could gain official or unofficial admittance to fashionable functions there was the tilt-yard and the various entertainments to be seen therein. It was not merely a matter of formal jousting in arms along a barrier, though that could be exciting enough. Sometimes there were encounters on foot, with combatants armed from the waist upwards only, striking at each other with sword or blunted spear across a barrier that was no more than a bar set between uprights. An elaborate joust at Whitehall was a sporting and social event honoured by the presence of the sovereign—in fact, a kind of Elizabethan Ascot—and an occasion for the display alike of athletic prowess and of elaborate and expensive equipment.

Arms, armour and the use of them were not only familiar to the eye, they formed subjects, in daily life as in the French camp scene in *Henry V*, for frequent and controversial conversation. The design, appearance and practical qualities of a man's armour could be discussed very much like those of a car today, and points of style and technique could furnish as much matter for argument and contradiction as those of a boxer or a racehorse, and

Jousters in lists, with the president of the festivities watching from his box, and elderly and critical spectators in the grandstands on either side.

for the same reason, since they were concerned with sport, and could be as hotly disputed by those who habitually watched the sport as by those who practised it. In such a state of things it would have been fruitless for any manager to scuffle through his combats on the principle that 'anything will do—they don't know any better out in front.' The fighting could not be expected to compete in quality with the combats of the tilt-yard or the platform of the professional 'prizer', but it must be good enough to pass muster with an audience reasonably critical in such matters, and in attaining this end the actor's skill might find itself much indebted to the author's ingenuity.

Looking for a moment at Shakespeare's handling of the matter, we find him, from the very outset, alive to the importance and value of variety. What one may call the Tybalt-and-Ajax technique, of writing a short and easy part for an accomplished swordsman, is employed again and again to good advantage, but in very different ways. Burgundy and Matthew Gough, in the First and Second Parts respectively of *Henry VI*, are characteristic examples, Burgundy having very little to say and Matthew Gough nothing at all. In modern editions, Burgundy's fight with York is taken away from him and given to Joan the Maid, but what the Folio says is 'Burgundie and York fight hand to hand. French flye.' The boy who played Joan had had two fights by this time in which to display his ability, and that would be quite enough for him. What the audience would want to see, in a play like this and in a theatre like the Rose on Bankside, would be a rousing hand-to-hand combat between two grown and active men, and here at last it comes. York, as a principal, would be able to fence and act, Burgundy would have been engaged for his fighting rather than his acting ability. Earlier in the play, Burgundy has been seen as an ally of the English, being later persuaded by Joan to come over to the side of France, and this circumstance would make him all the more suitable to be fought with and soundly beaten, in the last act, by one of the few surviving Englishmen. The simple patriotism of the average South Bank audience would welcome an energetic fight in which an Englishman beat a foreigner, and if the discomfited opponent had been represented as being not only a foreigner but a turncoat into the bargain, why, that was better still, and the wretch was getting no more than he deserved. After applauding that, the spectators would be quite content to let York return with a captive Joan and accept that she had been taken prisoner, since her supernatural protection had visibly failed her at the last. They had just enjoyed a really good fight, and a lesser one after it would be an anticlimax.

Quite possibly, the man who played Burgundy reappeared in the Second Part as Matthew Gough, who meets his death leading the troops from the Tower against Jack Cade's rebels. The little episode seems inexplicable until we look into the chronicles to find out just who Matthew Gough was. He was a Welshman, a captain of Talbot's who had distinguished himself in the French wars, and was appointed by Lord Scales to lead and marshal the hurriedly-mobilized citizens by reason of his valour, experience and military reputation. Quite obviously the mention of his name still meant something to a Shakespearean audience. Such a figure would be distinguished from the rest by being probably dressed in the nearest thing to complete armour that the wardrobe could provide, and the sight of his efforts, overthrow and death at the hands of his lighter-armed but more numerous opponents would be a spectacular effect quite different from the usual run of theatrical combats.

Conversely, there was another matter to be considered by Elizabethan managements and the authors who wrote for them. What was to be done about players who were good actors but not necessarily accomplished swordsmen? Shakespeare adroitly puts the Tybalt-and-Ajax technique into reverse and allows them to create the impression of being mighty warriors without having the awkward test of a visible stage-combat of full length to destroy the illusion. Austria, as we have seen, is killed off-stage. Heroes like Clifford and Warwick, in *Henry VI*, come in wounded to death, after terrific combats that we can believe in although—or is it because?—we have not been allowed to see them. Tullus Aufidius has to be a good actor if we are to see and understand his smouldering jealousy of Coriolanus, but it will be a sad come-down if their combat shows him to be nowhere near his rival in an assault-at-arms. If, after all, he can fight as well as act, there is an opportunity for a good spectacular combat to show as much; if not, a very few passes will suffice, because the author has arranged for some of Aufidius' fellow-countrymen to come in and second him—very much to his annoyance. It is they who can be the real fighters; when there are three or four to one against Marcius, the display bout can be fought between him and these 'extras', and if they are seen to be better swordsmen than Aufidius, it gives all the more point to the latter's anger at the time and his later resentment.

The same problem arises in *Troilus and Cressida*, over two different people. Achilles, in this play, must be represented as handsome at all times and stupendous in armour, and the part must be cast accordingly. If the best-looking actor available is unhappily not much of a swordsman, a single combat between him and Hector must be avoided at all costs, or it will raise a laugh and let the performance down. Shakespeare gets round the difficulty by bringing in a partially exhausted Achilles to whom Hector can courteously allow a breathing-space, a favour which he accepts, though with an ill grace, and he goes off without having to do any fighting at all in the sight of the spectators. When he and Hector meet again, Hector has taken off a good deal of his own armour preparatory to putting on the more splendid harness of a dead enemy (as Homer says he did, in the 17th Book of the *Iliad*), and it is with this disadvantage that he faces the armed Achilles and his followers and takes death from their hands.

The other character who has to have a military reputation made for him is Troilus himself. Though he is Priam's youngest son, we have already heard from Ulysses that the Trojans are beginning to build upon him 'a second hope as fairly built as Hector', but it is asking rather much of a young actor to make him put it to the proof by a series of successful combats, and the author knows it. What he does is to give us a series of rapid glimpses of him in action, either in his own person or in the reports of others, be they raging enemies, like Ajax and Diomed, judicious critics like Ulysses or heroic figures like Hector, who has time, among his own exploits, to see and applaud his brother's prowess. We see him challenging two opponents at once, and shortly afterwards organizing a rescue for Aeneas, who has been taken prisoner, and finally bringing to him, and to the surviving Trojans, the appalling news of Hector's death. It is here, in this extraordinary series of reported combats, that the omission or mishandling of them can irretrievably damage the climax of the play. Without them, and without the glimpses of Troilus that they give us, we can too easily conceive of him ending, as he is often played, in a storm of almost hysterical passion and grief. When, on the other hand, they are taken seriously, as they were meant to be, we can imagine a different and far more impressive ending. Troilus has lately lost his adored Cressida, now he learns that he has lost his heroic brother, and that is a loss that betokens almost unquestionably the doom of Troy. The worst has happened, but that is no reason to relax his efforts, and so he tells his men as he rallies them in the gathering darkness. The bad news will fly fast enough into the city, and will have its effect there, no one can question that, but it is not for him and his followers to add to the general grief. They can still fight on, and in so doing they may have the easier part. The youth whom we first saw as a lover very well qualified for the unpitying mockery of a Rosalind has been driven by despair and disillusion to draw out the best in his nature, and his last lines to his men, as they leave the stage, speak of hope, comfort and revenge. As with Romeo years before, Shakespeare has turned a lovesick youth into a stern and resolute man by stripping him of practically all that he has to live for, but where Romeo can rush headlong to death, Troilus has work to do, comrades to encourage, and a doomed city to defend. Our last impression of him should be one of nobility, but we need to see those battle-scenes, and to see them done convincingly, if we are to understand as much.

After all this evidence of Shakespeare's consideration for the players who were to present his battle-scenes upon the stage, we may be temporarily disconcerted by half a dozen lines in the prologue to the fourth act of *Henry V*.

> And so our scene must to the battle fly,
> Where—O for pity!—we shall much disgrace
> With four or five most vile and ragged foils,
> Right ill disposed in brawl ridiculous,
> The name of Agincourt. Yet sit and see,
> Minding true things by what their mockeries be.

Editors, commentators and writers on the Shakespearean stage have cited this passage as evidence of the author's dissatisfaction with the material at his disposal, without paying proper attention to the ordinary conditions of the stage, and the people who act upon it and write for it. To express a wish for a Muse of Fire, with all the appropriate appurtenances, in the opening speech of the play is well and good, but to run down the quality, appearance and acting efficiency of your fellow-players—which is what people are so ready to say Shakespeare is doing here—is to cry 'Stinking fish!' in a way both unprofitable and discourteous. If he had really had such a poor opinion of his stage-soldiers, he would have taken care to avoid giving them a chance of showing their ineptitude, not derided them and warned the audience that they were going to see a bad performance. One does not write that sort of thing about one's own colleagues—nor, we may justly assume, did Shakespeare. The company would not have let him include the lines, the actor playing Chorus would not have consented to repeat them—acting-editions are inclined to cut the two middle lines even now—and, if we are to imagine anything about Shakespeare from his own works and from what his contemporaries said about him, his own good-nature and artistic conscience would never have suggested he should write them.

Yet write them he did, and we should do well to look into the passage a little more carefully and see what they really mean. After all, how *does* he present Agincourt—the actual battle? Neither an Elizabethan nor a modern stage can convincingly portray a cavalry charge thrown into confusion by a hailstorm of arrows, and that was the essential feature—and everybody knew it—of the encounter. The author has been far too sensible to attempt the impossible, and what he has done, instead, is to create a sense of increasing tension by showing the conditions in both camps immediately before the battle. The French herald bringing his master's message of defiance, the Dauphin and his nobles talking of horses and armour and longing for the morning, the 'poor condemned English' huddled over their fires, all prepare us for the coming fight, and when morning comes we are given a further sight of the young king quietly putting heart into his companions by his own undaunted bearing, till he and his army leave the stage.

And then comes the only part of the conflict which the author allows the audience to see, the only scene in which Englishman and Frenchman are visibly confronted—the diverting but unedifying sight of Pistol taking a prisoner. It is a firmly-held theory among soldiers that practically all the rewards of war go to the wrong people, and the theory is gloriously illustrated by this scene, wherein a cowardly blusterer, with no valour and no French, counts on his bellowing and grimaces to counterfeit the one, and his delightful and disrespectful page to supply the other, and thus possesses himself of the person and potential ransom of a well-to-do Frenchman. Here, surely, is the episode for which the chorus-speech was apologetically preparing us. The scene is essentially 'brawl ridiculous', and Pistol in all his enormity is as vile and ragged a foil to the courteous, knightly king as author could provide or audience require. If Chorus has spoken his 'O for pity' lines with a smile of apology, instead of the customary note of regretful concern, we shall have been subconsciously prepared for this and all the readier to enjoy it, and to mind 'true things by what their mockeries be' with the greater ease when the mockery is unashamed, and not a serious effort which has fallen embarrasingly short of its purpose.

But perhaps the most curious of all Shakespeare's stage battles is the one in *Cymbeline*, the last play in the Folio and very nearly the last he wrote. After a march of the Roman and British armies in succession across the stage, in which Postumus is seen joining the British contingent in disguise, come the usual Alarums, followed by an elaborate and spectacular engagement, summed up in the words of the stage direction 'The battle continues; the Britons fly; Cymbeline is taken; then enter, to his rescue, Belarius, Guiderius and Arviragus'. The lines given to Belarius and his supposed sons are magnificently written for declamation:

> Stand, stand! We have th'advantage of the ground;
> The lane is guarded; nothing routs us but
> The villainy of our fears.
> Stand,—stand, and fight!

Then comes another stage direction, 'Re-enter Postumus and seconds the Britons; they rescue Cymbeline, and all exeunt. Then re-enter Lucius, Iachimo and Imogen.' The Roman general's words at once indicate that the tide of battle has turned against them and they must look to themselves, but how much would the audience understand of the confused and violent performance that had gone before? Shakespeare seems to have been well aware of this, and to have met the difficulty after his own fashion, simply and effectively, by writing a scene between Postumus and one of Cymbeline's lords, in which Postumus describes the event, and not only the event but the topography which made it possible and on which it all depended. The point was that the old man and his two sons stopped the flight of their fellow-countrymen by taking their stand in a sunk lane between two high banks of turf, and effectively blocking it. (The episode was to be found in Holinshed, or rather in Hector Boece's history of Scotland, translated by William Harrison and published as part of Holinshed's chronicle, and Shakespeare had simply transferred it to his Romano-British romance.) That sunk lane, and the banks of turf that made it so easy to defend, are practically unstageable, yet the position has to be made clear to the audience if the episode is to be included, and we may well admire the dramatist's ingenuity in handling it. The capture and rescue of Cymbeline himself are obvious enough, but the rest of the action verges on the incomprehensible and disconcerting unless an explanation is provided before we have had time to start puzzling ourselves over what was meant to be happening. The short scene with Caius Lucius has relieved most of the tension and shown the result of the action, and the time is ripe for a little straightforward explanation of the action itself, so Shakespeare puts it before us in the form of a timely narrative, and we are satisfied. It is a bold stroke, to have the action first and the explanation afterwards, but the author's technique and timing have been good enough to make it a successful one.

From the very beginning, then, of his dramatic career he seems to have had a clear eye for the effects he could obtain with his stage combats of one kind or another, and his methods of creating those effects have been varied and ingenious. The one thing he seems to have counted on throughout is that the fights should be taken seriously and carried out efficiently. His audiences, as we have seen, were qualified to be sharply critical of such matters, and we may take it that the players saw to it that their author and their public should not be disappointed. But from the author's point of view there was more to it than that. Fights in general could enliven the action, and please the audience as sheer exhibitions of skill, but it should be possible to make them do more. Properly sited in the dramatic development, they could be used to heighten character, particularly in the last few minutes of a historical play. Richard III refusing to withdraw from the field, but shouting for a horse to bear him once more against his enemies, and perishing after a terrific combat with his supplanter, can make that fight as effective as any dying speech; Richard II, fighting in his prison with a weapon snatched from the armed men who come against him, dies with a heroism he has never shown till now, and earns the tribute 'As full of valour as of royal blood' from the mouth of his murderer; Harry of Monmouth, saving his father from the sword of Douglas on Shrewsbury field, does away with the estrangement that has grown up between them, but the most interesting and impressive examples are to be found in three of the last great tragedies, and it is worth while considering them in some detail.

The assault-at-arms in the last scene of *Hamlet* is perhaps the best-known combat in all Shakespeare, but nevertheless there are some difficulties about this particular fight. To begin with, it is not fully established what weapons are to be used. Quite often one sees it fought with those useful cross-hilted swords of a type best described as Costumier's Nondescript—to Suit Any Period—and the technique is that of the modern foil, 18th-century attitudes and all. Sometimes the swords are of the same type, but held sabre-fashion, so that there is a great deal of fear-some clashing of blades and not so much risk to the person of either combatant. Again, it is not infrequently done in reasonably good imitation of Elizabethan rapier-and-dagger play, but with the cup-hilted rapiers of the 17th century rather than the open-hilted weapons of the 16th.

There are two main drawbacks to this, one being aesthetic and one practical. To take the first, we find from early treatises and miscellaneous allusions that rapier-and-dagger play, though widely taught, was not regarded as a polite accomplishment. One learnt it, sure enough, and used it in private duels and miscellaneous brawls, but one did not talk about it or display it in public, and it seems to have been looked upon as useful but rather low. Hamlet gently deprecates Osric's reference to it as one of Laertes' accomplishments, and Pompey, in *Measure for Measure*, speaks of 'Master Starve-lackey the rapier-and-dagger man' among the dubious characters whom he has met in jail and recognized from the old days when they were customers at Mistress Overdone's bawdy-house. Moreover, from the practical point of view, it was a style of fight in which it was practically impossible to exchange weapons in the course of the contest, as the action of the play requires.

The orthodox type of formal sword-play was the 'fight at single rapier'. It occupied the main part of the fencing-master's curriculum, and was explained at great length in the various treatises devoted to the sport, and it was the style most likely to be employed in a demonstration bout before a fashionable audi-ence like that of the Court of Denmark. The practice of suddenly seizing one's opponent's rapier-hilt with the left hand was not only possible but quite common, and fencing-masters described and illustrated various ways of doing it. The only answer to it, to avoid disarmament, was to repeat the manoeuvre oneself at the same time, with the result that each party would lose his own sword but fall back holding his adversary's weapon in his left hand, from which he would change it rapidly to his right and fight on.

All this fits in admirably with the stage direction in the Folio, which calls expressly for 'Attendants with foyles, and gauntlets,' and with the course of the fight as indicated in the dialogue. Laertes has been a little over-confident in his own skill. Before he knows where he is, Hamlet has gained the first hit and, a few passes later, the second. The king is losing confidence in him, and has frankly said so. Obviously the swordplay is getting wilder and more confused, and Osric has to proclaim 'nothing, neither way'. It looks very much as if Laertes, with his sudden cry of 'Have at you now!' were deliberately attacking before the signal to recommence had been properly given. A fencer may still be checked by the referee for being 'too quick off the mark', and it is at precisely such a moment, when taken at a disadvantage, that an Elizabethan swordsman might be expected to bring his gauntleted left hand into play and catch hold of the weapon that had just wounded him. The fact that the king's next line is 'Part them, they are incensed,' is sufficient indication that there is no question of challenging the hit by an appeal to the judges. Hamlet is counter-attacking at once, and is giving as good as he gets. It is only the collapse of the queen that prevents the bout from developing into an unseemly-looking brawl—if indeed it has not already done so. Both combatants have drawn blood, and are very far from the formal, slightly stilted courtesy with which they began.

So much for the fight as set forth in the First Folio, and consequently in most modern editions of the play. If that were all, there would be nothing to hesitate about, but it is not. The Folio was published in 1623, but two quarto editions had appeared some years before that. The first, a notoriously muddled and corrupt text, appears to be based on somebody's recollections of the play in performance, and in the account of the fight it corresponds with the Folio. This is likely to have been based on the script used in the theatre as a prompt-copy, so we may reasonably assume that it represents the duel as fought on the stage when the play was produced in Shakespeare's lifetime. The Second Quarto, on the other hand, appeared in 1605, and the late Professor Dover Wilson argued most persuasively that it was based on Shakespeare's original manuscript. And here, with quite embarrassing clarity, the stage direction specifies rapiers *and daggers* as the weapons brought in by the attendants.

What is one to do about this? The change of rapiers can hardly be brought about when each man's left hand is already occupied with a dagger. As a deliberate manoeuvre it is already out of the question; as a theatrical contrivance it becomes much more elaborate, involving an actor's accidental dropping or deliberate abandonment of his own weapon before he can catch hold of his adversary's, and runs the risk of appearing clumsy and absurd. We look to see what sort of stage direction the Quarto uses to denote it, and find there is none at all. The omission is ascribed by Dover Wilson to a 'scoundrelly compositor'—rather an illogical excuse, in view of the Professor's insistence, in other places, on the accuracy of this particular text—but a textual variation later on, either overlooked by the editor or tacitly ascribed to another misdeed on the part of the compositor, may provide a more reasonable explanation. Where in the Folio, and in the later texts, we find Laertes telling Hamlet that

> In thee there is not half an hour of life;
> The treacherous instrument is in thy hand
> Unbated and envenom'd,

the reading of the Second Quarto is 'in *my* hand'. Laertes is still holding the sharpened, pointed weapon, and the exchange has never taken place at all.

This puts a different construction on that final passage-of-arms. Stung by Laertes' unexpected attack, and by the smart of his wound, Hamlet has rushed in and counter-attacked Laertes hard enough to wound him—mortally, as it turns out—with the blunted weapon of the fence-school. Such things could happen, we know from contemporary allusions that they occasionally *did* happen, and the remarks of Laertes can be taken as meaning that his unfair attack, wounding and enraging Hamlet, has brought about his own death. That, we may take it, was the meaning of 'I am justly killed with mine own treachery' and the later confession that 'the foul practice hath turned itself on me'. Violence of that sort, it would seem, was not unfamiliar to Tudor audiences, and the author may well have intended it in the original draft of his play. After all, it would be no worse than the positively idiotic end of the villain in Cyril Tourneur's *Atheist's Tragedy*. This gentleman is preparing to behead his falsely-accused nephew, but 'in lifting up the axe, knocks out his own brains, and staggers off the scaffold', retaining coherence enough, however, to make a dying confession of his misdeeds.

On the other hand, the Chamberlain's Men were not that sort of company, and *Hamlet* was not that sort of play. One can easily imagine protests at rehearsal, on the lines of those made to Peter Quince in similar circumstances in *A Midsummer Night's Dream*. 'There are things in this play will never please', says Bottom, and instances the fact that Pyramus may alarm the ladies by drawing a sword to kill himself. Burbage may have found it necessary to say very much the same thing. The fight must be made less of a duel and more of an exhibition bout. Hamlet must not forfeit the sympathy of the audience by losing his temper and bruising his way to victory (any leading actor might well be emphatic about this). The author must do something, somehow, to avoid this awkwardness, and obligingly enough, with the minimum of textual alteration, the author does. The new version is written into the prompt-book and into Laertes' part, but not into the author's own personal copy—a point which is forgotten when this is the copy chosen, later on, to be sent to the printer. This is all conjecture, admittedly, but it is a conjecture that tallies closely enough with Dover Wilson's suggestion and with the available evidence.

Edgar's two fights in *King Lear* are ingeniously contrasted.

The first is a crude rough-and-tumble affair, when in his disguise as a peasant he defends his father against the braggart Oswald and kills his adversary with a cudgel, but in the second he appears armed and helmed, his face apparently hidden by a visor, and challenges Edmund with all the formality of chivalry. There are no horses and no lances; otherwise it is almost as elaborate in preparation as the trial by combat in *Richard II*, and this time it is allowed to go on to its due conclusion. Here, again, Shakespeare manages to link the combat with the dramatic situation and the character of the participants. The very fact that the challenger has to be asked his name, quality and reason for appearing in the lists calls forth an impressive answer,

> Know my name is lost,
> By treason's tooth bare-gnawn and canker-bit,
> Yet am I noble as the adversary
> I come to cope.

Indeed, it does more than that, for it calls forth the best qualities in the villainous Edmund. He has behaved most treacherously to his father, his brother and his king, he is carrying on an intrigue with the wife of his immediate commander and another with her widowed sister, he has just sent out instructions to have Lear and Cordelia murdered in their prison, but when he is faced with a sporting challenge, as now, he takes it like a sportsman. He has a perfect right to refuse a combat with an opponent who will not give his name and rank, but he waives that right because he likes the look of him and considers that his words show 'some say of breeding'. Wounded and dying, he is still chivalrous, asks who it is that has overthrown him and gratuitously adds, 'If thou'rt noble, I do forgive thee.' Just before this, a passage of eight or ten lines between Albany and Goneril has diverted attention to them, and has given Edgar time to get his helmet off, so that when he turns round in answer, the legitimate brother is at last revealed to the illegitimate, and Edmund learns, to his relief, that he has not been struck down by an inferior but by his equal in blood, his own father's son.

The more formal and ceremonious the preliminaries, the more

dramatically important is the fight itself, and the more impressive the tension at the close of it, because that very formality makes it clear that not only Edgar, Albany and the herald, but all the surrounding warriors, regard the trial by battle as a solemn appeal to the judgement of God, and its result as the Divine answer. So, in his turn, does Edmund himself, making free admission of his guilt and concerned only to know the name and rank of his conqueror. Edgar's first words in reply, 'Let's exchange charity', are a clear indication that he is not to speak in self-congratulation. 'I am no less in blood than thou art, Edmund,' is not a boast, but a reassurance. It is just the thing that Edmund wants to hear, and Edgar knows it. Next moment, with the words 'thy father's son', comes another reflection. It is not all Edmund's fault: if their father had not been promiscuous, there would never have been an Edmund at all, and all this would not have happened. It is not in sententiousness, but in awed reverence, that he speaks the famous lines

> The gods are just, and of our pleasant vices
> Make instruments to plague us.

Only with the entry of the faithful Kent do we realize with a shock that the fight and its result have done another thing, and have occupied our attention so exclusively that for a time not only Albany and his officers, but we in the audience, have completely forgotten King Lear.

Different again, but just as important dramatically and psychologically, is the last fight of Macbeth. The very first mention of him in the play describes him in battle

> Disdaining fortune, with his brandished steel
> Which smoked with bloody execution,

but he is never actually seen fighting until the very end. And even there his first fight, the little passage-at-arms with young Siward, must be a whirlwind affair, like Romeo's killing of Tybalt, over as soon as it was begun. The very ease of it heightens Macbeth's desperate frustration. His castle is assailed, his wife has destroyed herself—choosing a most inconvenient time to do it—he himself is assured that no man born of woman can harm him, so there is nothing for him to do but kill others. He need not trouble even to defend himself. Life, for him, is no longer worth living, yet he is condemned, it would seem, to an unavoidable immortality.

Then, suddenly, he is confronted with the bereaved Macduff, and makes an unexpected admission,

> Of all men else I have avoided thee,
> But get thee back, my soul is too much charged
> With blood of thine already.

It is not, surely, the witches' warning that he has in mind, not the armed head in the cavern telling him to beware Macduff, but the thought of the man's wife, children and dependants, murdered on his own instructions. No man, he is assured, can kill him, but here is a man whom he finds he himself would prefer not to kill. Even when attacked, he tries to stop him, to tell him that he is wasting time and energy on a man with a charmed life, but in reply comes the shattering news that the charm is valueless by reason of Macduff's unnatural birth.

His first reaction is a profoundly simple one—that of the indignant child or sportsman who considers he has been cheated and cries out, 'It's not fair—I shan't play!' It is so spontaneous that he can hardly have realized that he is doing the almost unmentionable thing, and refusing a challenge. Once again, Elizabethan scenic conventions must have helped the situation here. Without a localized, painted setting of castle or battle-field, the audience can forget that an assault is supposed to be in progress, and need be neither confused by the presence of other combatants nor disconcerted by the lack of them. There may be a battle going on somewhere else, but in this place, and at this moment, two men are facing each other in a personal enmity that nothing but death can end.

Macduff's taunts bring Macbeth to himself again, and here, with a sudden reversal of feeling, he finds himself almost freed from his despair. He has relied on the witches and the prophecies, and one after another they have failed him. The adversary before him is the one man he has been told to beware, and, by virtue of his birth, is the one man who can kill him, and Birnam wood has come against him to Dunsinane. The impossible things have happened, and this is the end. And yet, when all is said and done, there is one thing left for him to rely on. It has yet to be seen whether he or Macduff is the better fighter. Magic is laid aside, seconds are out of the ring, it is not spells, but his shield and his valour, that are to defend him now, even as, a long time ago, they won him the good name he has cast away. Irrelevancies are done with, and once more 'disdaining Fortune' he can go, almost with a sense of relief, to the business he understands.

This fight, then, must be tremendous, and exciting enough for Macbeth to regain our sympathy in the course of it. There was a wonderful and elaborate encounter that was said to have been worked out originally by, or for, Irving for use in this play and in *Richard III*, and was handed down in the theatre for many years. It involved the dropping of a sword, its recovery after an attack with the shield used as a weapon, and at the end a slow stab with a dagger at the base of the throat, driven inexorably down against the frantic pushing of gradually-weakening hands. The late Baliol Holloway knew it and used it in both capacities, as victor when he played Macduff to the Macbeth of—I think—Edmund Willard in 1921, and as victim in his own production of *Richard III* nearly ten years later. The effect was unforgettable, and on each occasion the protagonist appeared to gain an unexpected nobility by the vigour and valour of his end.

X

Armour on the Shakespearean Stage

What sort of armour did Shakespearean actors wear for their battle-scenes and single combats? The evidence is only slight, it must be admitted, but there is enough of it to supply matter for consideration and possible conjecture. Specific references to armour on the stage are remarkably few in Shakespeare's work, with the exception of one play which stands alone in such matters, but there are one or two instances in plays by his contemporaries which have an interest of their own and may also indicate what audiences of that day might expect to see.

The one direct piece of evidence is Henry Peacham's famous drawing at Longleat, with its group from the first scene of *Titus Andronicus*. Here, fortunately, we have no less than six out of seven figures wearing armour of sorts. Titus himself, as befits a Roman warrior and father of five-and-twenty sons, has a laurel wreath, a venerable beard, a classical-looking cuirass and buskins, and a military cloak knotted on the left shoulder, and carries a tasselled spear. Two of his sons, behind him, carry halberds and wear half-armour, but of differing types. The one on the extreme left wears something very like the normal equipment of an Elizabethan infantry officer. His breastplate is crossed by a distinctive scarf knotted on the right shoulder, his one visible arm shows that he is wearing complete arm defences, shoulder-pieces and gauntlets, and about his neck can be seen a series of lines indicating the presence of a gorget, the hinged rings of which rise close up to the jaw-line. Instead of a helmet, he wears a tall plumed bonnet in Spanish style, with narrow brim, full bag-shaped crown and strongly contrasting hatband. His sword, with its curved blade and pistol-like grip, has an Oriental look about it, but weapons of this scimitar form were familiar among the seafaring men of all nations, particularly in the Mediterranean. He is unarmed below the waist, but appears to be wearing very full breeches, boldly striped, cut after the fashion of the Swiss mercenary infantry who played such an active part in the wars of 16th-century Europe.

His companion's armour is even more interesting, since, though lightly indicated, it shows features that the artist was highly unlikely to have imagined and must therefore be assumed

Light-armed foot-soldier wearing a headpiece such as Peacham has attempted to illustrate, not very successfully, in Plate III.

to have seen and drawn upon a living actor. The breastplate in two parts, with its chevron-like effect in front and its suggestion of bold fluting, belongs quite unmistakably to the late 15th-century German type commonly known as 'Gothic', and the difference between the arm-defences and those of the other figure suggest very strongly that the arms and cuirass are all *en suite*. Armour of this type was completely out of use by 1595, the date on the drawing. A hundred years earlier, when Wohlgemut and

Pleydenwurff were illustrating Hartmann Schedel's *Nuremberg Chronicle,* it was still quite familiar, and well enough understood to be expressively depicted in some of their woodcuts, but when an anonymous illustrator was devising or cutting the block for the portrait of one Sysillius, king of Britain, in the 1577 edition of Holinshed (a portrait used again for Cnaeus Trebellius some 50 pages later on), that lugubrious monarch appeared to be dressed in open umbrellas. The principles and design of Gothic armour were not, by that time, generally understood or accurately remembered, so it would seem that what Peacham saw must have been a real Gothic cuirass of about 1480, that had found its way eventually to a theatrical wardrobe. There seems to be an attempt to suggest that the actor is wearing some rather curious looking leg armour, with laminated 'sabatons' on his feet, and his headpiece is not a fashionable hat, like that of his companion, but an infantry steel-cap of the kind known as a combed morion. It is not very well drawn, but that kind of helmet is very difficult to draw in such a way as to indicate the characteristic fore-and-aft cock of the brim, and the sharp angle of the upturned points. The comb can be clearly seen, running across the skull from front to back, into the shelter of the plumes which would be set in a small tubular socket at the nape of the neck, where the comb ran down to meet the brim. The chin-strap, covered with small plates of metal, is just visible, apparently hanging loose behind the angle of the wearer's jaw.

The other three men, Tamora's two sons and Aaron the Moor (an unquestionable blackamoor in the true sense of the word) are all wearing reasonably accurate Roman-type cuirasses and buskins like those of Titus, and here we may note what first looks like an anomaly in the dressing of the cast. The Goths and the Moor are clad in Roman armour, while two out of the three Romans are not, and yet, at the same time, the general effect looks somehow quite right. The explanation seems to lie in the impression conveyed at first sight. The bearded, laurelled patriarch with spear and mantle is obviously a Roman father coming home in triumph, and the groups at each side of the picture represent the two contending nations. The captives and

III Detail from Henry Peacham's sketch (1595) of a scene from *Titus Andronicus*. The foremost figure is wearing a reasonably well-drawn 15th-century cuirass, while his companion wears something more like contemporary body-armour but is girt with a curved sword of the type associated with the East. Such out-of-date oddments would still form very useful additions to an Elizabethan stage-wardrobe.

the Moor are the enemy, the foreigners, the thwarted invaders, and so it is proper that they should be dressed after a slightly exotic and unfamiliar fashion, even though it would really be more appropriate on their conquerors. These represent what one might call the home team,—the forces of Rome, of civilization and order as opposed to barbarism—and therefore they are accepted the more easily as sympathetic characters if they look like the audience's ideas of St George in a pageant, or recollections of Essex in the tilt-yard or Ralegh coming home from an expedition abroad. It is less important that they should look like real Romans than that they should be recognizable at once as national heroes, and such modern or near-modern armour as was available would therefore be appropriated to them. The Roman-looking armour of Titus and the Goths would not be difficult to contrive, and might quite possibly be made of moulded leather. It is not, in this play, put to the test in actual battle, but has only to look the part and create its effect thereby. Indeed, after this particular scene all the characters except Lucius (probably the gentleman in the good Elizabethan half-armour and the smart hat) would discard it for the remainder of the play.

His companion's out-of-date armour tempts one to a little far-fetched but not impermissible conjecture. Was it perhaps something that was so old and obsolete that it was not usually accepted as costume at all, but hung somewhere in the tiring-house or its purlieus as a stage property—used, perhaps, to dress the stage when it was necessary to suggest either a general's camp or a hero's tomb? Various casual references suggest that Shakespeare was familiar with the sight of battered armour hanging rusty and neglected on a wall. Not only is there the famous reference to 'our bruised arms hung up for monuments' in the first half-dozen lines of *Richard III*, but Ulysses, reasoning with Achilles in the third act of *Troilus and Cressida*, puts it to him that to live on a reputation for prowess in the past

> is to hang
> Quite out of fashion, like a rusty mail
> In monumental mockery,

and the same comparison occurs in *Measure for Measure*, where Claudio declares that Angelo, in sentencing him, has revived some obsolete

> penalties
> Which have like unscour'd armour hung by the wall
> So long, that nineteen zodiacs have gone round
> And none of them been worn.

We know from the pages of Stow's *Annals* that the merchants on the upper floor of the Royal Exchange sold, among other things, 'old armour and new', and it looks as if what was really too old and out of date for practical use in the field, or even preservation as municipal or parish property, might be acquired cheap for theatrical purposes. The *Titus Andronicus* drawing illustrates a production by Henslowe's company, which played at the Rose and had Alleyn for its leading actor, but there must have been old armour available in or about the property-room of the Chamberlain's Men as well, because when Shakespeare had transferred his services to that company he wrote at least two scenes in which it had to be used. One is the scene in *Richard III* that occurs immediately after the arrest and summary execution of Hastings. Richard and Buckingham enter, as the Folio stage direction has it, 'in rotten armour, marvellous ill-favoured', as if they had been compelled to take extreme measures in a sudden emergency, and thus give to the Lord Mayor and his followers the impression that the execution was practically forced upon them in the national interest. Hall, Grafton and Holinshed say that they actually did receive the City authorities 'in old evil-favoured briganders, such as no man would ween that they would have vouchsafed to put on their backs, except some sudden necessity had constrained them'. Even in the late 15th century the Tower was a storehouse of early armour, and Richard and Buckingham had created an effect of sudden alarm by hastily equipping themselves with 'museum pieces', as being the nearest available protective clothing. The point would be effective theatrically, and would make itself clear to the spectators whether or not they had read their Hall or

Holinshed, but it was not essential, and Shakespeare makes no express reference to it in the text, so that it could be omitted if the company's wardrobe did not contain anything really rusty and shabby enough to serve its turn.

Some years later he has a use for it again. When trimming up someone else's uneven play of *Pericles, Prince of Tyre,* and incidentally rewriting the three final acts completely, he put a certain amount of his own unquestionable work into the first and second acts as well. Usually this takes the form of odd lines or short passages here and there, but the scene between the shipwrecked Pericles and the fishermen who cheer him with food and clothing has the mark of Shakespeare from the fishermen's entry to the end, and includes an episode that is not found in the narrative on which the play is based. The fishermen are shown drawing up their net, exclaiming at the weight of their catch and finding with an oath of disappointment that ''Tis turned to a rusty armour.' Pericles eagerly examines it, and recognizes it as his own, and his father's before him, and in the course of the act he presents himself in it, all rusty as it is, to joust at the birthday festivities of the princess of Pentapolis. He does not have to fight in it on the stage; the six champions merely pass across in turn, the squire of each presenting his master's shield for inspection by the princess, who in her turn describes its device, until Pericles, having no squire, presents his own. The semi-heraldic parade is decorative in action and must have formed a connecting link, to many beholders, between classical antiquity and their own time. Pageant shields with elaborate and allusive devices or 'emblems' were familiar objects of the Elizabethan tilt-yard (Shakespeare and Burbage were commissioned to devise and paint one respectively for the earl of Rutland in 1613). Hall had recorded very much the same thing in describing some of the elaborate 'housings', with their mottoes and devices, used by Henry VIII. The whole custom was reminiscent of various legends of chivalry, while the classical scholar would remember that Aeschylus had done just the same thing in *The Seven Against Thebes*.

As the other champions are not seen to fight in their armour, but have to dance in it at the subsequent banquet, there would be no need to have it made of metal, and it would probably be of gilded leather or some kind of stiffened fabric. The rusty harness of Pericles, on the other hand, would be subjected to closer scrutiny, and would have to sound metallic when first dragged on to the stage and handled by its owner and the fishermen. Its very realism, rustiness and weight would contrast strikingly with the splendour of the rival champions—a contrast emphasized by the caustic comments of the noble spectators—and the actual fighting is tactfully arranged to take place off-stage, the triumph of the stranger being announced merely by 'Great shouts within', hailing 'the mean knight'. At the banquet, the five competitors are expressively told by the king to dance 'Even in your armours, as you are addressed', but Pericles takes no part in this performance, and when in his turn he is made to act as partner to the princess, we may assume that their contribution to the dance would be something formal, stately and discreetly short. There is no occasion for Pericles to appear in armour again, but the old suit out of the property-room has once more come in handy, and has even had quite an important part in the development of the play.

For the many battle-scenes in the various Histories and Tragedies, it would be enough for some of the actors to wear the ordinary back-and-breast and a steel-cap, either the morion of the pikeman or musketeer or the close-fitting burgonet with its hinged cheek-pieces, that gave protection to head and face and yet allowed the wearer to speak freely and audibly when he wished. The burgonet, by the way, is almost the only type of helmet mentioned by Shakespeare by its technical name, and is certainly one of the most practical for stage purposes, being quickly put on or removed and allowing comparative ease of speech throughout, which a helmet with a visor does not. The word 'beaver', technically the lower part of the visor, is used by Shakespeare to denote the visor as a whole, notably in the description of the Ghost in *Hamlet*, whose face was visible and recognizable because, as Horatio reports, 'he wore his beaver up', and in the passage in *Henry V* in which Grandpré, describing the state of the English army before Agincourt, says expressively that

> Big Mars seems bankrupt in their beggared host
> And faintly through a rusty beaver peeps.

It is possible that Edgar, appearing in arms at the end of *King Lear*, was originally played in half-armour with a close-helmet, the visor of which, when raised but not turned right back, would leave his mouth free to speak his lines while still keeping his face unrecognized in its shadow. One wants, dramatically, the effect of a masked, faceless figure uttering the lines in which he declares his nobility but not his name.

Another virtue of the burgonet as a stage helmet would be its broadly classical outline. Some examples deliberately imitated Greek types, the long peak over the brow being drawn out in a continuation of the curve of the skull and comb, so that on occasion it could look quite passably Roman if required, and if worn with the right sort of cuirass and buskins. The *Titus* drawing has shown the difficulty of deciding just how Roman Shakespeare's stage Romans are likely to have looked. The evidence of Holinshed's woodcuts is too widely varied to be of much help. One never knows what engagements the many battle-pieces were first designed to represent, since they are used with glorious inconsequence over and over again in widely different contexts. The Romans who are shown invading Britain look like Spanish infantry in the New World, firearms, morions and all, while later on we find Renaissance round-hose and half-armour confronting unmistakable Romans on the battlefield of Tewkesbury. It is safest to assume that Holinshed's publisher and the average Elizabethan theatrical manager pursued the same policy of illustrating such episodes as they chose with such material as they could lay their hands on.

The suicides on the battlefield in *Julius Caesar* are notoriously difficult to negotiate successfully, partly because they are so numerous and come so close together, and partly from the difficulty of stabbing oneself, or being stabbed, efficiently in armour. One has either to take it off, or to feel carefully for a joint where the sword might go in, and either process is apt to take time and hold up the action when everything calls for speed. Some actors in these scenes have been known to ignore the armour and seem to stab themselves unashamedly through the breastplate as if they were wearing no body-armour at all, but this is hardly an improvement and sometimes raises a laugh. Brutus, if he is quick about it and has someone in the wings to help him, has just time to get out of his breastplate in the course of the short scene between Lucilius and Antony, and can appear exhausted and practically unarmed among his 'poor remains of friends' for the last scene, but Cassius and Titinius have no such opportunity, and are actually in combat at the beginning of the scene in which they kill themselves.

It is an awkward point, and Shakespeare takes good care to avoid any such risk in his next Roman play, when he depicts the suicide of Antony. This time there is no mistake or possibility of confusion. Eros is summoned to unarm his master, and given plenty of time in which to do it, while Antony is speaking. More, he is able to pick up the armour and take it away, avoiding the problem of how to get it off the stage afterwards without an anticlimax. The author has arranged for it to be out of sight and out of mind before leading the audience on to see the loyalty of Eros in his death, and his master's tragically bungled attempt to follow him. It is a wonderful antithesis to that earlier moment in the act, when Antony was shown putting on his armour for a different and more successful battle, and Cleopatra was enthusiastically lending a hand, doing something up wrong, so that Antony had gently to contradict her, generally hindering Eros in his task and finally being immensely pleased with herself at having fastened one buckle correctly. Consciously or not, Shakespeare has well illustrated the proverb quoted by king Ahab to Ben-Hadad of Syria, 'Let not him that girdeth on his harness boast himself as he that putteth it off.'

It takes a writer of high quality to introduce successfully into a dramatic scene an effect of ordinary, almost comic frustration. Macbeth, faced with the desertion of his thanes, the near-madness of his wife, the news of an advancing English army and the knowledge that whatever happens life will never be worth living again, calls impulsively for his armour. There is no prospect of immediate hand-to-hand combat, and Seyton his attendant tries to say so, but Macbeth will not be denied. In a few moments he is trying simultaneously to put it on, give orders, snap at the man who is doing his best to arm him, and talk to a somewhat apprehensive Doctor about the general situation, and he is not successful. Probably, on the Jacobean stage, the armour would be a simple back-and-breast, but even with this, the straps cannot be properly fastened if the wearer refuses to stand still but keeps on turning to speak to this person or that. In a moment Macbeth loses all patience, shakes himself free and storms away, calling for the armour to be brought after him. In other circumstances the episode might be a matter of pure farce and an opportunity for a fine display of comic fury and exasperation, but not with this man, whose nerves are frayed threadbare by what he has gone through, and whose infernal guarantees of safety will soon be failing him one by one. It is a brief but tragic sign that his own self-control and efficiency are deserting him as his friends and nobles have done, and that the end may be very near.

Quite different is the description of a similar situation in another play. *Troilus and Cressida* has an unusual amount of armour in it, and treats it from a rather unusual standpoint. Many of the references to it have a particular significance for hearers who know what it is to put on armour, and to watch other people doing so. At the very beginning the Prologue enters in armour, instead of the traditional black cloak, and claims to be

suited
In like conditions as our argument,

an intimation to the spectators that they are going to see a play about warfare. (Ben Jonson, though ready to be sharply critical of his friend and former colleague, was not above borrowing a good idea when it suited him, and brought in an armed Prologue in his turn when the Children of the Chapel Royal produced his *Poetaster* in 1601.) The opening line of the play itself, 'Call here my varlet, I'll unarm again,' shows that Troilus has entered in armour, and as nobody does what he asks, he stays in armour until the end of the scene, when he goes out to 'the sport abroad' with Aeneas, who must likewise be armed for the field. In due course they come back in formal procession after the morning's fighting, and pass across the stage, with Hector, Paris, Helenus and Antenor, all obviously armed—Pandarus draws attention to the battle-scars on Hector's helmet—and followed by others, whom he caustically dismisses as 'chaff and bran, chaff and bran, porridge after meat!'

This is all rather different from the military parades to be seen in some of the other plays. Even if the actors are only wearing half-armour (which is most likely; leg-armour was mostly restricted to mounted men, and is troublesome to walk in, even if it is an exact fit), there must have been quite a lot of it, and it would have to be good, if the play were being presented before an audience of courtiers who were accustomed themselves to wearing armour in the tilt-yard under the approving eye of the queen.

Only those who had themselves worn armour, and knew the technical difficulties and exertions of getting into it or out of it, would fully appreciate the passage, a little later, in which Ulysses describes, to Agamemnon and the aged Nestor, Patroclus' ribald imitation of Nestor 'arming to answer in a night alarm'. There might well be something broadly amusing in the spectacle of a flustered old gentleman putting on armour in a hurry, but the few lines that follow take the matter a good deal further for auditors familiar with the details of its construction.

> And then (forsooth) the faint defects of age
> Must be the scene of mirth; to cough and spit
> And, with a palsy fumbling on his gorget
> Shake in and out the rivet,

says Ulysses, and in those words he describes one of the first and most uncomfortable stages in arming for the field.

The gorget is made up of two or three rings of steel, fitting one inside another and fastened by rivets to vertical straps of buff-leather, so that each has a limited amount of play within the one below it. On the left side they are hinged, on the right they fasten by springing a hole in the front portion over a stud on the rear one. This would all be comparatively easy but for the fact that below the actual neck-rings the gorget finishes in two broad plates, one covering the upper part of the breast and the other protecting the cervical vertebrae. Both these extend sideways over the shoulders, and on the left side they are fastened by a fixed rivet, while on the right a keyhole-shaped slot in one plate has to go over the head of a rivet fixed in the other. The construction is ingenious, and these lower plates perform a very important function, since the shoulder-straps of the cuirass pass over them and they distribute its weight among the shoulder-blades, collar-bones, breastbone and the upper part of the spine, instead of concentrating it agonizingly on the two points immediately beneath the straps. At the same time, the difference in plane between the gorget-rings on their hinge and the two lower plates with their connecting rivet means that the piece cannot be opened very far in the process of putting it on or taking it off. Because of its height, the wearer has to raise his chin and bend his head slightly backward, while forcing the gorget open as far as it will go and trying to slide or scrape its narrow opening sideways across his neck. From the position of his head, he cannot see what he is doing, from the position of his hands he can get very little purchase, and when once he gets the opening past his Adam's apple, it has a tendency to spring shut and catch a small fold of skin or neck-muscle between two plates, which is agony. For someone with a beard of any size, the hazards must be still more numerous and painful.

Then comes the business of fitting the hole over the stud on the central neck-rings. When wrestling with these, one almost invariably has to put one's thumb or fingers over the rim, between one's neck and the gorget, to drag either the one plate in or the other one out. Still, of course, one has to do it by feeling alone, and the assistance of another person is very little use here. For the straps and buckles of the rest of the armour it is welcome, but for this particular semi-strangling operation the wearer must usually minister to himself. It is with a wonderful feeling of relief that one hears the click, and feels the sudden comfort, that shows one has aimed aright and fitted hole over stud without being able to see either.

With the last rivet, the one on the shoulder-plate, assistance is possible and advisable; otherwise it is extremely painful for the groping thumb at the edge of the plate. Once again, one has to fit a hole one cannot find over a stud one cannot see, and then keep the plates firmly pressed together while sliding the upper one along so that the narrow part of the slot comes under the mushroom head of the rivet and the two plates are held firmly together. An incautious movement, or a weakly tremulous one made while the rivet-head is still under the broad entry-hole of the slot, will make the plates spring apart again, and 'shake in and out the rivet' exactly as Ulysses describes. To imitate a doddering old man going through these contortions, half-throttling himself with the gorget-rings, getting his beard shut in between overlapping plates and finally having failure after failure with the shoulder-rivet, would be an unkind and disrespectful performance, but would be likely to make Achilles laugh, and to commend itself to the younger and still active members of a fashionable, courtly audience.

In the scene of the friendly bout between Hector and Ajax, it is noticeable that the two champions take no part in the preliminary discussion. Ajax has a few lines at the very beginning of the scene, but does not share in the series of compliments and kisses with which his companions greet the newly-arrived Cressida. Quite possibly he is occupied, during this little scene of gallantry, with the business of putting on his helmet, or having it put on for him by his attendants. During the conversation between Aeneas and the Greek nobles, Hector and Ajax will be standing armed, helmed and silent, probably with visors closed, and marked out conspicuously, by their armour and their immobility, from the fashionable spectators. There is something very impressive, and rather sinister, in the sight of a man moving in armour that fits him, especially if his face is hidden by a visor so that one cannot tell if, or how far, he is affected by ordinary human emotions. There is something of the same feeling in *Richard II*, when

Mowbray and Bolingbroke are about to enter the lists at Coventry, but though they are armed, they are not helmed until the very last moment, and have a good deal of conversational oath-taking and leave-taking beforehand. Hector and Ajax are handled differently and more impressively, moving against each other like machines or monsters until the stopping of the trumpets gives the signal for the seconds to part them. Visors go up, or helmets off, and they are human again, visible and exchanging courtesies like ordinary mortals.

Two touches in the plays about Henry V as prince and king would probably rouse appreciation in the minds of some of the ex-soldiers who were in London in large numbers at the end of the century, having obtained their discharge after service under Essex at Cadiz or in his ill-fated expedition with Ralegh to the Azores. Even now, indeed, they have a familiar ring. Dr G. B. Harrison has said of Hal's comparison of majesty to

> a rich armour worn in heat of day
> That scalds with safety

that, 'Anyone who has served in a tank in a tropical climate knows the significance of that line,' and the Constable of France and the duke of Orleans, talking casually of armour and other things on the night before Agincourt, maintain that the English must be stupid by nature, or they would run away, and 'if their heads had any intellectual armour, they could never wear such heavy headpieces'. One can imagine the sardonic approval of the discharged soldier to whom grumbling at the weight of his equipment had been a matter of course throughout his military career. There is as yet no known, decisive evidence, but to many scholars there seems to be a very strong likelihood that Shakespeare wrote of certain military situations, and military sentiments, from his own personal experience.

These practical considerations of armour may give an added interest to a couple of passages in plays by Shakespeare's successors. In *The Two Noble Kinsmen* (by Beaumont and Fletcher, with assistance, it is generally held, from Shakespeare), Palamon and Arcite, the two kinsmen of the title, are estranged by their rivalry for the love of the same lady. Palamon has been imprisoned, but has escaped and is hiding in a wood near Athens; Arcite has been banished, but has returned to court in disguise, and has won the favour of duke Theseus. In these rather improbable circumstances they meet and arrange to fight a duel to the death. Arcite first procures a file for Palamon's chains, and undertakes to come back with swords and armour for both of them. Their conversation, when he does so, is a fascinating mixture of extravagant compliment and cheerful technicality about the kit necessary for a sporting event. First, of course, they contend in courtesy, each wanting the other to have first choice of armour. Palamon eventually chooses a suit, and Arcite helps him to put it on. When one realizes that the awkward gorget has to go on first, it becomes quite clear that Arcite is carrying out the necessary adjustment while Palamon is standing rigid—the only thing to do—and asking a natural question:

> Pray thee, tell me, cousin,
> Where got'st thou this good armour?

Arcite replies cheerfully,

> 'Tis the Duke's,
> And to say true, I stole it—do I pinch you?

It sounds as if Palamon had uttered a sound that might be either a chuckle or a strangled noise of protest at being nipped in the neck by the gorget-plates, but he is in haste to say 'No', and presumably the body-armour comes next. Arcite's reaction, as he picks it up, is a perfectly natural one; 'Is't not too heavy?' while one can imagine Palamon settling it on to his shoulders as he replies,

> I have worn a lighter,
> But I shall make it serve.

If the back-and-breast feels unduly heavy on the shoulders, the thing to do is to strap the girdle as tightly as possible, so that the cuirass rests on the hips—or rather the padding of the garments worn over them—instead of being a dead weight upon the shoulder-straps. Sure enough, Arcite's answer is 'I'll buckle't close.'

Then comes a rather surprising remark, 'You care not for a Grand-guard?' and it is not surprising, on the other hand, that Palamon replies, 'No, no, we'll use no horses.' The grand-guard was about the largest, heaviest and most elaborately shaped of the various reinforcing-pieces used under highly formal conditions in the tilt-yard, where both combatants were on horseback and considerations of mobility could be practically disregarded in favour of absolute protection. For general combat purposes, and on foot at that, it would be infinitely more trouble than it was worth, and its production at such a moment would be so absurd that we may wonder how, or why, it has got into the scene at all.

It depends, perhaps, on the means by which Arcite has brought combat armour for two persons on to the stage. If he has had to carry it all in his arms—with a couple of swords to manage as well—one simply does not believe in his burdening himself with anything so manifestly unsuitable. On the other hand, there is an air of high comedy about the scene which would be well supported if he were to make his entrance trundling an assortment of armour in a wheelbarrow. Armour of high quality, such as the duke's would be, comprised a wide range of spare parts or alternative pieces devised specially for one or another type of combat, and it would be quite plausible for Arcite to find, at this stage, that he had inadvertently brought a piece that neither of them could possibly want, and characteristic of him to continue his courtesy to the point of absurdity by politely offering it to his opponent. It is just in that spirit that Palamon receives it, chaffingly pretending to believe that Arcite would rather fight on horseback, but next moment the waist-buckle is being tightened, he is asking for his helmet and deciding not to wear plate arm defences, but to be content with gauntlets alone. It is always at the elbow and knee joints that unfamiliar armour is likely to hamper one's movements, and there was always the possibility that the available stage arm-pieces might not fit the actor who played Palamon. Body-armour, as a rule, can be adjusted to this figure or that by altering the straps, but that for the arms and legs is jointed with rivets, and is consequently unalterable.

The authors do not make the mistake of repeating their effects. Now that it is Palamon's turn to arm Arcite, his reactions are quite different. He finds himself reminded of the armour Arcite wore on the day when they both distinguished themselves at the beginning of the play, and they talk of that early battle, and Arcite's horse, and once again each praises the other's prowess. Palamon has a momentary fear that he may have done up one piece rather too tightly, but Arcite reassures him, and in a moment they are giving each other the duellist's formal salute and preparing to kill or be killed.

The little scene has made one further point, which is worth bearing in mind. Palamon has asked for his helmet, and it is obvious that by the time he says, 'How do I look?' he has put it on, but it does not seem to hinder his conversation in any way. That suggests that the helmet in question must be a burgonet, a popular type already described, which provided just this advantage and was accordingly very suitable for stage use, both here and in Webster's bloodthirsty tragedy *The White Devil.* In the lists or in the field it could be worn either open-faced or augmented with a separate piece called the buffe, which was clipped on to the cheek-pieces and secured with a strap behind the head. This, when fixed in place, had the effect of turning an open-faced helmet into a 'close', or visored one, and as it could not be raised, like a pivoted visor, it was often made in several overlapping pieces which were held up by spring catches but could be allowed to drop, nearly to mouth level, by pressure on the appropriate studs. We have already seen how the word 'beaver' is loosely used by Shakespeare to denote the upper part of the visor, or the visor as a whole. It is more properly used to denote the lowest part, that covers the cheeks and chin, and where Webster uses the word, in the last act of *The White Devil*, the details of Brachiano's murder are readily clarified if we take the word as denoting a detachable buffe.

The whole arrangement is most ingenious and plausible. Brachiano has arranged an elaborate 'combat at barriers' for the entertainment of the foreign ambassadors who have come to attend his wedding. In due course the stage direction announces his entry 'all armed, save the beaver', and as the scene goes on, one of the conspirators against him 'sprinkles Brachiano's beaver with a poison'. Brachiano's last words in the scene are 'Where's our beaver?' as he goes out to put it on, and the next scene begins with what must have been quite a spectacular theatrical contest, as the stage directions run, 'Charges and shouts. They fight at barriers; first single pairs, then three to three.' When it is at its height, Brachiano enters in agony, shouting for an armourer and crying, 'Tear off my beaver,' a thing which he himself could not easily do with his steel-gauntleted hands. It is taken off, he declares that 'The helmet is poison'd' and has the armourer sent off to torture, and finally he dies raving, being strangled, for good measure, by his two murderers disguised as Capuchin friars.

The important point is that with a burgonet and buffe, such a murder would seem quite convincing to a Jacobean audience. Any fencer will know the necessity of having a chin-pad fixed in the lower rim of his mask. Such a feature was equally necessary for a buffe, and would be covered with soft leather or velvet. If this were saturated with a suitable poison, just before the wearer put it on and took violent exercise, he would have it uncomfortably close to his mouth and nose in the confined space of a practically closed helmet, and the audience would readily accept his subsequent convulsions as a very natural consequence. It is an extravagantly sensational murder, but staged in that way it would seem quite disconcertingly easy to carry out, and the audience would be all the more impressed with the verisimilitude of the whole affair.

XI

Financial Embarrassments

There is generally something rather amusing about incongruity, especially if it takes the form of dignity or elegance in difficulties. The more absurd the difficulties, the readier are we, as spectators, to regard the dignified or elegant sufferer with mirth, tolerance and a certain amount of sympathy. Orsino and Olivia cannot restrain their laughter at the plight of Malvolio in the last scene of *Twelfth Night*, but we can be sure, from what they say, that it is kind laughter, and Theseus, at the end of *A Midsummer Night's Dream*, makes it clear to Quince and his Dramatic Society (who take themselves very seriously) that he appreciates their efforts and has enjoyed their performance. Shakespeare knew all about this principle, as he knew about most things. His two best farces are full of it. Ford and Falstaff, and the increasingly frantic young gentlemen of Ephesus and Syracuse in their Comedy of Errors, work it up to a pitch of frenzy, to the delight of all beholders, but we are perhaps inclined to overlook it when it occurs in tragedy or in what Beaumont and Fletcher, a few years later, were to classify as tragi-comedy. All the same, it is quite unquestionably there, and two whole plays turn on the grim difficulty of paying back money that one owes (a practice of which both Falstaff and Pistol disapprove on principle) or of getting it back from the people to whom one has lent it—a difficulty summed up by Polonius in the succinct and embarrassing truism that 'loan oft loses both itself and friend'.

One such play, of course, is *The Merchant of Venice*. We have got so used to the very title that the look of it on the printed page, or the sound of it when spoken aloud, no longer calls up thoughts of great trading figures in a great commercial city. The phrase has become a *cliché*, and to the present-day reader or hearer it means Shakespeare. To the Elizabethan, on the other hand, it most probably meant Money. Merchants had money, Venice lived by money, a Venetian merchant who was important enough to have a play written about him would almost certainly be represented as having a very great deal of money, and his fortunes, or at least his fortune, might be expected to have a great deal to do with the story of the play. So, perhaps, might the Elizabethan Londoner have instinctively thought when he saw the name of the play on a bill posted outside the theatre, or heard it announced from the stage as a forthcoming attraction to be presented in a few days' time. And we cannot say, on reflection, that he would have been far wrong.

From its very beginning the play declares itself a comedy, and we must not be too solemn in our contemplation of Antonio and his business associates taking themselves very seriously—two of them, at least—and talking shop. As for what happens next, we have become so used to considering it as poetry that we run the risk of forgetting how much there is in the situation that is richly comic as well. Bassanio's difficulty in getting to the point, the speed with which the older merchants take themselves off as soon as they see what is coming, the readiness of Bassanio's own friends to hurry away till they can meet at dinner-time and hear how he has got on—all these different degrees of embarrassment are there for our diversion, if we have the wit to notice them, and underlying them all there must be a certain embarrassment in Antonio himself, who cannot fail to see what all this is leading up to. His friends have been lecturing him on the rashness of some of his recent ventures, and here is an investment which is almost certainly not going to pay a dividend at present.

Sure enough, there is soon no doubt about that. Ostensibly, Bassanio has promised to tell Antonio about his projected visit to a lady, but he begins instead to make a somewhat shamefaced confession of his late tendency to live beyond his means. The more serious he is about it, the more obvious is his embarrassment, social as well as financial, and it is with a certain wicked relish that we can see—as can the unfortunate Antonio—what is coming. Not only does it mean that Bassanio is not in a position to pay back what he has already borrowed; it is a sure sign that he wants to borrow more. This whole conversation has become so familiar to us from our schooldays that we have got into the way of regarding it as just Shakespeare instead of noticing how true to life it is. It is a regrettable fact that the best safeguard against being asked to pay back money that you owe is to borrow more from the same source, as long as you can possibly do so, and the art of living more or less on credit, or at least at the expense of one's acquaintances, has long been a matter for light comedy (think of Wodehouse's Mr Ukridge) or for scarifying indictment such as Thackeray has given us in the terrible thirty-seventh chapter of *Vanity Fair*.

Familiar, also, is the next turn Shakespeare gives to the transaction. It is a slight embarrassment to Antonio that—for reasons we have seen—he has no ready money available. Still, he is ready to take the indiscreet step of pledging his credit. He promises to look round and see where he can raise the money, and rashly advises Bassanio to do the same. In Antonio's mind, this would mean approaching some of his fellow-merchants, the Salanios and Salarinos of Venetian commerce, but to the man about town the natural place to borrow money, after having approached one's personal friends, is the Ghetto, and thither, accordingly, he goes.

We do not see the opening of the negotiations. They are in full swing when the third scene introduces Shylock the Jew, and it is clear at once that poor Bassanio has done the wrong thing, and that there may well be trouble. Shylock is going appreciatively over the main points of the agreement—three thousand ducats—a loan for three months—and (probably with quiet, lip-licking relish) Antonio bound. The audience may well begin to be apprehensive about Antonio's feelings when he learns what his young friend is letting him in for, and Bassanio himself seems none too easy in his mind, from the way he seems to be fidgetting and nervously seeking the right words in which to frame his downright question. 'Can you—er—help me—are you able to oblige—can you let me know if—er—?' That, in modern parlance, is the meaning of that 'May you stead me? will you pleasure me? shall I know your answer?' though it is apt to come out in performance as another piece of just Shakespeare, rather than a clear indication of the anxiety of that worried young man.

It is perfectly natural for Antonio, as soon as he comes on to the stage, to stand aghast at the sight of what Bassanio is obviously doing, and what company he is keeping. His horror keeps up the comedy of the situation, and Shylock's little soliloquy, as if he were taking the audience into his confidence, gives time to get the maximum value out of it. The scene now takes a turn that has more than a touch of Galsworthy about it, with a dignified and sympathetic character being led by the conventions of his class into a line of thought and conduct that he himself finds vaguely distasteful, but it is just that dignity and conventionality that move us, at the same time, to smile at his embarrassment. Antonio has been led into a false position, and finds himself committed to asking a favour from someone with whom he would not think of doing business in the ordinary course of things, but with an obvious effort he puts as good a face on it as possible, and speaks to Shylock politely though without enthusiasm about the proposed bargain.

It is all the more awkward for him, and the more diverting for the audience, that Shylock leaps at the opportunity of doing business with a great Christian merchant, and launches out, with sniggering familiarity, into a long and not very edifying story out of the Old Testament about Jacob getting the better of Laban his father-in-law over some spotted sheep. Antonio does not particularly want to hear a Stock Exchange story of the 'Well, you see, there were these two Jews' variety, in defence of a type of business that he disapproves of, and though he is still courteous—with increasing difficulty—he is not going to pretend that he is amused, so he soon tries to bring matters to a head by a direct question in his turn, 'Well, Shylock, shall we be beholding to you?' Even here, in his choice of words, he is tactful enough to make it clear that it is he and Bassanio who will be under an obligation to Shylock if he does them this favour, but the point does not seem to be appreciated. Instead of giving a direct answer, and getting the whole sorry business settled as soon as possible, Shylock piles on the agony by a long diatribe against the way in which he is ordinarily treated by Antonio and his friends, and rubs in the fact that it is they who are now coming to him for favours, as if Antonio had not just made that particular point himself.

Antonio's reply to this is surely misrepresented when, as so often, it is delivered in tones of arrogant indignation. It is rather the voice of a man who is determined to be honest and trying as hard as he can to be still courteous and reasonable. There must be no mistake; his views on usury have not changed, and this transaction is not to be made the pretext for familiarity, for further business or for expecting any alteration in Antonio's customary attitude to interest and those who ask for it. The original audience for this play was largely a mercantile one, and its members would be very well qualified to enjoy Antonio's awkward predicament and at the same time to admire his behaviour in it, while relishing Antonio's discomfort at being drawn deeper and deeper in. He has tried to make himself clear without being actively impolite, and in return this impossible person first taxes him, most unjustly, with 'storming', and follows it up with the unctuous assurance 'I would be *friends* with you, and have your love'—a state of things which Antonio is desperately anxious to avoid. What with his suppressed frenzy and Shylock's enthusiastic fawning, the situation is attaining a degree of comedy that is appreciably near to farce, particularly as Bassanio by this time is quite outclassed and tongue-tied, and is hanging about in increasing uncertainty whether he will get his money or not.

At this point he hears something that he can understand, though it seems quite incredible. The Jew has actually said something about not taking any interest. It is Antonio's turn to be tongue-tied now. Shylock assures him that he is doing it out of kindness, and Bassanio eagerly agrees—it looks as if he were going to be justified, after all, in his choice of a source of supply. Next moment the heads of the agreement are being outlined—a straight-forward loan on Antonio's note of hand alone, with a penalty clause so fantastic that nobody can be expected to take it seriously. The only one who *does* take it seriously is Bassanio, who is not a business man, and therefore has his objection promptly brushed aside by the more experienced speculator. Antonio is so relieved at his release from a highly disagreeable situation that he is not only quite polite to Shylock, but speaks gratuitously well of him behind his back, and concludes the act with a couplet that shows him to be in better spirits than we have seen him yet. The financial problem has been satisfactorily settled for the present, and we can turn our attention all the more freely to the progress of Bassanio's courtship.

The very fact that we have found ourselves amused by Antonio's embarrassment in the first act makes us all the readier to applaud the way he bears himself when he has got into real trouble in the third and fourth. He may have been embarrassed at having to do business with someone very much outside his usual circle of acquaintance, but the strictness of principle that caused that embarrassment is now seen at its best, upholding him unflinching in his adversity. It is interesting, and characteristic of him, that when matters have gone very wrong indeed, and the Jew is pressing for specific performance of his contract, he dismisses at once, on business grounds, the optimistic suggestion of Salarino that the duke will denounce the contract as bad in law. Bard-baiters have been very ready to do so in later years, disregarding the author's carefulness in meeting this argument by letting Antonio explain the matter. To deny a foreigner his rights in favour of a Venetian citizen would not only be a breach of law, but a breach that would seriously impair the commercial reputation of Venice in the eyes of the many nations who normally engaged with her in commerce. It would be both unjust and injudicious, and that is that.

Shylock, in his turn, says the same thing in a few passionate and almost unanswerable lines,

> If you deny me, fie upon your law;
> There is no force in the decrees of Venice!
> I stand for judgement; answer, shall I have it?

It is the duke's turn, and the turn of his whole stately Court, to be embarrassed now. Nobody can deny the facts, and nobody tries to. Antonio has signed the bond, has had the money, and must be expected to pay the penalty if strict justice is to be done, but the duke is not prepared to give a ruling on his own authority. He is prepared to dismiss the court unless he can get a definitive legal opinion. The disguised Portia's first appeal is not a sentimental one, hardly, indeed, an emotional one, but rather an attempt to refer the matter to common humanity and common sense. This failing, she presses the doctrine of specific performance to the uttermost, and Shylock is caught in his own trap.

Now—*pace* those many scholars who are so ready to decry the Christian's treatment of the defeated Jew—common sense and common humanity take over, in the place of strict justice, and Shylock sees the answer to his earlier rhetorical question 'If a Jew wrong a Christian, what is his humility?' In terms of justice, Portia points out, his offence against Antonio is punishable by the forfeiture of all his property and, if the duke so choose, his life. Her advice to him is not, this time, to show mercy, but to beg it, but before he can do so, that mercy is immediately shown. Shylock's life is granted him, and while half his property must go to Antonio, the injured party, there is a hint that in respect of the other half he may get off with a fine if he behaves himself.

More than one production of recent years has shown that Gratiano's running commentary is much more amusing, and less ill-natured, when made from the public seats of the court—possibly the gallery over the stage—than when delivered conversationally at close range. His remarks come out like the extravagances of a heckler at a political meeting, or a football spectator apostrophizing a referee, and while they may voice the feelings of the extremists in the audience, they contrive also to make those feelings more than a little ridiculous. Also, more subtly, they enhance the effect of what follows, when Antonio, the man most intimately concerned, is asked in his turn, 'What mercy can you render?' His answer is considerably clarified if one colon in the Folio text is replaced by a comma, so that it reads:

So please my lord the duke and all the court
To quit the fine for one half of his goods,
I am content, so he will let me have
The other half in use, to render it,
Upon his death, unto the gentleman
That lately stole his daughter.

It is meaningless to make a complete pause after the word 'content', as if the sentence were to end there. It is not for Antonio to be content if the State decides not to fine Shylock at all. That colon is surely no more than a breathing-pause before he says, as clearly as he can, what he really wants. What he is saying is that if the duke will leave Shylock in possession of half his property, he himself will be content to hold the other half in trust only, and to deliver it to Shylock's son-in-law Lorenzo when the time comes. We must remember that Antonio believes himself to be practically bankrupt from his shipping losses, and is in urgent need of capital if he is to recover his position.

All things considered, Shylock has come out of the affair with better fortune than he might have done if the laws of Venice had been observed as strictly as he had claimed to observe his bond. As it is, half his estate is out of his hands, but is to be administered by Antonio in the interests of Jessica's husband; the other half, instead of being confiscated by the duke, is still his own, and it in turn is secured to his son-in-law. The money at any rate will stay in the family, and that means much. His only pecuniary loss (apart from the jewels pilfered by Jessica) seems to be the interest he might have secured on future loans. As a Christian—albeit a compelled one—he will be debarred from the practice of usury, and will have to depend on judicious investment, such as the financing of commercial ventures like Antonio's, if he is to emulate Marlowe's Barabas in *The Jew of Malta* and 'becomes as wealthy as he was'. But there are possibilities, and he still has some capital, and may well conclude with Sir Hugh Evans that 'seven hundred pounds and possibilities is good gifts'.

From the injudicious borrower we may turn to the injudicious lender, from the professional moneylender to the enthusiastic amateur. The career of Timon of Athens, as presented by Shakespeare, corresponds in general outline with that of more than one Elizabethan gentleman whose brief period of splendour and hospitality had ruined his estate and driven him from court

English nobleman in richly-furred gown and high 'copatain' hat. This would be the type most nearly approximating, in the eyes of the original audience, to Shakespeare's Timon in the period of his prosperity.

into the shadows of obscurity. Timon is not one to say, 'I will be assured I may, and that I may be assured, I will bethink me', as Shylock does. When he sees a need, he supplies it as a matter of course, with a loan or a gift, and with no more pause for reflection than Sheridan's Charles Surface or Goldsmith's Good-natured Man.

The play is in many places a good deal subtler than the casual reader may be inclined to think. In performance it offers a dangerous temptation to producers to overdo the unworthiness and *grotesquerie* of Timon's assorted friends, flatterers and parasites, regardless of the fact that in so doing they are belittling Timon's intelligence and making him lose the sympathy of the audience at the very outset. Lord Timon, as some of the characters call him, is presented as the Elizabethan playgoer's idea of what a lord should be—a person of impeccable taste, a patron of art and literature, a benefactor to the deserving, and a generous and hospitable friend to practically everyone. The poet and painter whose conversation begins the play may not turn out to be very estimable citizens, or very desirable friends for Timon, but there is nothing in their lines as yet to say so, or to suggest that the poet is not a good poet, or the painter a good painter. Indeed, the poet's description of his allegorical composition is a bold indication of the course the play itself is to follow, but it is apt to go for nothing if the speaker is made, from the outset, consciously absurd. On the contrary, the better they all appear to be in their professions, the more they can contribute to the impression that Timon surrounds himself with people who are among the best in their kind.

That, indeed, is what makes the discovery of their shortcomings so appalling. When Timon comes in listening to a message on behalf of his friend Ventidius, who has got into debt, it is surely by way of reassurance, not of self-glorification, that he says:

> Well,
> I am not of that feather to shake off
> My friend when he must need me. I do know him
> A gentleman that well deserves a help,
> Which he shall have. I'll pay the debt, and free him.

Even in the act of well-doing, he manages to fit in a compliment to the character of the recipient, and to follow it up with an injunction to come and see him with a view to further help until he is once more able to support himself. Quite obviously Timon does not regard himself as anything out of the common. He takes it for granted that anyone else in his position would do the same as a matter of course. Next moment he is pacifying an indignant old gentleman whose daughter wants to marry one of Timon's attendants, and agreeing to settle on the bridegroom an amount equal to the dowry of the bride, and then he passes on to speak words of encouragement and commendation to poet, painter and jeweller in turn. There is no exaggeration or obvious fawning in their conversation or behaviour; they say the sort of things that Shakespeare would say himself in similar circumstances, and indeed *did* say, and say in writing, when dedicating his two great narrative poems to the Earl of Southampton. Patrons expected it as a matter of course, and artists and craftsmen duly supplied what was expected of them. So far, the scene is running a perfectly natural course, and ends with Timon inviting the Senators and Alcibiades to dine and warning the craftsmen not to go away till he has had time to look at their work properly after dinner and 'thank' them for it—and they will all know very well what that means, and that it will be well worth their while to stay.

All this is particularly interesting because this aspect of Timon, and a good deal of what happens in the succeeding acts, is not to be found in Plutarch's account of Timon, which Shakespeare would have come across when getting up his material for *Antony and Cleopatra*. It comes out of a dialogue of Lucian, and makes one wonder whether perhaps Shakespeare knew a little more Greek than Ben Jonson's famous remark would give him credit for, or whether he had access to a colleague who was something of a classical scholar and could prime him, on request, with the sort of thing he wanted to know. (This would explain, incidentally, the very close parallels with Homer to be found in various parts of *Troilus and Cressida*, notably in the matter of Hector's death.) There is no direct evidence, but we have not to look far to find someone who might fill the bill. Thomas Heywood, at one time a Fellow of Peterhouse, Cambridge, had been actor and playwright for the Admiral's Men, with whom Shakespeare apparently started. Like Shakespeare, he had had Southampton for patron, and at some time in his career he read and translated Lucian, for he published a verse paraphrase of this particular dialogue, among others, a good many years after Shakespeare's death. It is tempting to think that the two had been on congenial terms, and the very fact of their patron's fall from favour at the time of the Essex rebellion had given them something more in common, as this very play can show. Heywood is just the sort of man to whom one would turn to ask what sort of curse an angry Athenian would launch at someone he was abusing. How else would Shakespeare have lighted on the expressive but unusual 'Would thou wouldst burst!' which is in fact the first word spoken by Peisthetairus in the *Birds* of Aristophanes? It is a rude but eminently suitable expletive for Shakespeare's purpose, and Heywood was just the sort of man to provide it. He was a classical scholar of somewhat Bohemian habits—it was said that he wrote his first drafts on the backs of tavern-bills—he knew more about the story of Timon than did most people, and the *Birds* is one of the two plays in which Aristophanes mentions Timon by name. We may perhaps imagine the two old colleagues exchanging professional gossip in a hostelry, the one talking about his current work on Lucian's Timon, the other asking if that is the Timon he has come across in Plutarch's life of Antony, and learning that there is more, and more dramatic material, about him than Plutarch gives, and considering the possibilities of it. He might well come back, later on, with a request for a good mouth-filling objurgation for an Ancient Greek to use, and get one from the text in which the scholar was looking up his Timon cross-references. The fancy is far-fetched, perhaps, but not entirely impermissible.

To return to the play itself. In a later scene, the Folio direction runs:

> Hoboyes Playing lowd Musicke.
> A great Banquet serv'd in: and then, Enter Lord Timon,
> the States, the Athenian Lords, Ventigius which Timon
> redeem'd from prison. Then comes dropping after
> all Apemantus discontentedly like himselfe.

The order of events is both significant and effective—first the sound, then the splendour of the banquet, then the entry of Timon with his illustrious guests and finally, as a sharp contrast, the sour-tongued philosopher 'dropping after all' and characteristically acting as a critical, chastening commentator from the corner where he sits at his separate table making his 'austerity meal' of roots and water and summing up Vegetarian Socialism in words of one syllable, 'Rich men sin, and I eat root.'

There has been no need for caricature. Quite obviously this sort of thing cannot last, and the remarks of Flavius the steward have made it clear to the audience that supplies are running out. When he tries to say as much to his master, he has no more success with him than the old steward in Hogarth's *Marriage à la Mode*, and indeed there is a strong suggestion of the 18th century as the play moves on to a note of grim comedy with its realistic study of a creditor who feels that he had better take steps to get his money back before his fellows begin to send in their bills, since there is obviously not enough for everyone. It is very regrettable, and practically modern.

So is the progress of events as the play goes on, with its set of semi-comic characters bringing about a tragedy. The harassed steward coming in with his hands full of unpaid bills, the easy familiarity of the different moneylenders' clerks, all coming together on the same errand at the rumour that Timon is in difficulties, Timon's annoyance at being buttonholed by duns on his arrival home from a morning's hunting—and in front of Alcibiades and the others, too—and the way in which he takes his steward to task first for letting such a thing happen at all and then for not warning him beforehand that it was imminent—all these things have their parallels in many a story of present-day business failure. Even at such a moment, when the creditors' servants are being hustled aside and promised an explanation when dinner is over, Timon addresses them as 'good friends' and gives instructions for them to be well entertained, while he goes away to see to his guests and incidentally to be told the main fact of his near-bankruptcy.

When we see him again, his reactions are those of many a financially-embarrassed nobleman, and still, as such, a matter for comedy, but not for long. We smile when he blames Flaminius for not having told him the position long ago, and pooh-poohs the idea that he himself has never consented to listen, but his next order has a special and a specially shocking sound to a Shakespearean audience. He says, in so many words, 'Let all my land be sold'. But land, to the Elizabethan Englishman as to the Victorian Lady Bracknell, was a combination of asset and responsibility. A man's landed property, however small, was something to serve and to preserve at all costs, and he would be as reluctant as Naboth to part with the inheritance of his fathers. (Shakespeare had expressed this clearly enough in *Richard II*, when the news of the king's farming-out of the Crown lands came to darken the last hours of John of Gaunt, and the actual sale of land was like paying current debts out of capital, a surrender of resources that could never be recovered again.) If Timon's command brings a shock to the audience, the steward's reply brings a still greater shock to Timon. ''Tis all engaged, some forfeited and gone,' he says, and his master's reaction is a cry of incredulity and protest, 'To Lacedaemon did my land extend!' It is of no avail; the reply comes respectfully and regretfully, but it puts the matter beyond doubt, and Timon protests no further. It takes him some time to recover, and he can only protest feebly against Flavius' elaboration of the position, but when he speaks again he shows himself at his best.

There is no easy optimism like Antonio's certainty that his ships would come home a month before the day; still less is there any vague Micawber-like assurance that something will turn up. He grounds his confidence on his absolute trust in the loyalty of his friends, and tries to encourage the unhappy Flavius by his insistence. Indeed, in a moment he is almost glad of his misfortunes, because they will enable his friends to show friendship in their turn, and get all the more credit for it. Servants are sent for, and told to go to this man and to that, applying for 50 talents from each, and the steward himself is to approach the Senate for a government loan on the strength of Timon's past services to the state. (This, by the way, is the first reference to Plutarch's story of Timon's having put Athens under an obligation by his services in the Peloponnesian war.) There is a slight check here, as it turns out that Flavius has tried that course already with no success, and he describes his interview with the appropriate government department so expressively that it raises Timon's spirits still further. He seems to cheer Flavius up by making light of it, suggesting flippant and uncomplimentary reasons for the Senators' parsimony, and—most helpful of all—instantly suggesting a different line to pursue. Flavius is to go to Ventidius and ask him after all for those five talents that he was so ready to pay back at the dinner-party. By this time, Timon has practically forgotten his own shock and the peril of bankruptcy that threatens him; his main concern is to comfort and encourage a faithful servant by assuring him of his continued confidence and lessen his sense of despair and impotence by giving him something practical to do.

The whole scene, in fact, is a piece of fine dramatic construction. We have seen Timon's prosperity, his indiscreet generosity and his heedless disregard of such warnings as come to him from churlish philosopher or faithful servant. Now, almost in the exact middle of the play, he has been faced with the fact, shattering, unpalatable and at the same time undeniable, that his debts are enormous and his assets negligible, and instead of being abased by the discovery he rallies under the shock and shows the strength of mind, and consideration for others, that were so clearly a part of him in his first appearance on the stage. The man who could say to an artist, 'I like your work, and you shall find I like it,' has every reason, when admitting his unwisdom, to claim that 'Unwisely, not ignobly have I given,' and to draw comfort for himself and others from the recollection.

Unfortunately, we are apt to overlook practically all of this because of our ingrained idea that this is a bad play, unworthy of Shakespeare and therefore written, for the most part, by somebody else, except for the purple patches, which were associated by Swinburne, in an impassioned moment, with 'the triune furies of Ezekiel, of Juvenal and of Dante'. It is a theory that has seriously affected the earlier part of the play and obscured its importance. That done, we are left with Timon's invective in the wilderness, and may justly feel that if this is what the play is about, we have taken a long time getting there. So we have, if we persist in closing our eyes, ears and intelligence to the actions and passions—and particularly the lighter touches—of these very realistic scenes.

But worse lies ahead. After this central moment when Timon reveals his real strength of character, he is kept off the stage for several scenes which are decried as being insufficiently Shakespearean, possibly because they are for the most part in prose, more probably because they are disconcertingly realistic and diverting. Timon's high-society friends are not savagely caricatured—that is perhaps the trouble—but they *are* presented as embarrassingly familiar, ordinary human beings. At the Globe, Timon would be accepted as a kind of poor man's Lear, suffering from the ingratitude of people whom Bankside spectators would recognize as being the sort one might only too easily find anywhere. Lucullus is obviously a kindly, garrulous old gentleman, childishly eager for the present he thinks Timon's boy has brought him, and really shocked and disappointed to find the great man falling so far short of expectation as actually to be asking *him* for a loan! In his exuberance at the sight of Flaminius he has bidden him 'very respectively welcome' and called for wine, but by the time it comes he has learnt the awful truth and, it would seem, is so upset that he takes a hasty drink himself without offering any to his visitor at all. He begins to compliment and flatter Flaminius—who obviously knows what is coming and is not very responsive—and is just getting into his stride when he realizes that the servant who brought the wine is still standing there listening for all he is worth, so that he must break off and send the man about his business and start all over again. There is a wonderfully persuasive note about his confidential man-to-man frankness, with its assurance that 'thy lord's a bountiful gentleman, but thou art wise, and *thou* know'st well enough (although thou com'st to me) that this is no time to lend money—especially upon bare friendship without security'. He would rather not be so unkind as to refuse, so he hopes Flaminius will understand and (for a consideration) go back and pretend not to have seen him. When Flaminius indignantly rejects the money, and all his careful diplomacy is wasted, he is understandably very cross, and brings the interview to an abrupt end. It is a delightful little scene, and very rewarding to the character actor (or, as Shakespeare and his colleagues would call him, the Humorous Man) who plays it.

Lucius, the next beneficiary whom we see, is also a pleasant and amusing person, though of a different type. He is quite clearly something of a tuft-hunter, and anxious to show his companions how well he knows the great Lord Timon, but his tuft-hunting is as naïve as was Lucullus' eager acquisitiveness. First he assures the strangers that there simply cannot be anything in the rumour they have heard about Timon's insolvency—he is far too intimate with him, he implies, not to have known if there had been—then he uses the news about Lucullus to declare how differently he himself would have responded to any such appeal, and one cannot help admiring the ingenuity with which he meets that appeal when it comes a few lines later. In both these scenes we are induced to forget their serious consequences for Timon because of our sudden interest in the embarrassment of two successive characters, not so estimable but just as human as he. One has extricated himself from the difficulties of repayment by urging the calls of prudence, the second presents himself frankly as the victim of circumstances. A third is shown armed in righteous indignation, now because Timon has not made his application to other people first, and then, still more emphatically, because he has.

There is usually something rather diverting in the sight of a gentleman making frantic efforts to avoid paying money that he ought to pay, and to justify himself at the same time, and this act shows us in rapid succession three different ways of doing it. We are not, however, shown the refusal of Ventidius, which would be very hard to explain or excuse, nor do we see Timon's own reception of the news that, now that he has no money, he may reckon himself as having no friends. What we are given is a bitter echo of the opening scene, with a crowd of people waiting for Timon's levée, but instead of clients, tradesmen, senators, friends and miscellaneous hangers-on they are moneylenders' representatives eager for the chance to present their statements of account. The servants assure them that the great man is not coming out that day, Flavius the steward is caught trying to slip past them unobtrusively, and declares that he has come to the end of his service, but these precautions are rendered all unavailing by the sudden appearance of Timon, raging and defiant. The duns leap at the opportunity and rush in with their various bills, Timon receives them with a curse, and is gone again, and one of the moneylenders' servants observes philosophically that their masters may 'throw their caps at their money', for obviously there is little or nothing to be got from this particular debtor.

But, in a moment, Timon is seen working out a new idea, almost oblivious of the presence of his steward. The mere circumstance of being invited to yet another dinner should raise his failing credit in the eyes of his former friends, and, sure enough, it does so. They come along, eagerly chattering about this recent appeal and deciding it must have been merely a test or a hoax, and are just beginning to compare notes on the amounts they were asked to lend when he himself is among them greeting them as courteously and airily as if nothing so sordid as a request for money had ever come between them. The banquet is brought in, Timon utters a long and elaborate grace, and it is gradually borne in upon his hearers that he is saying some very peculiar things indeed. The more orthodox and devout he is in his elocution, the more effective is the slow realization of his sentiments, culminating in the sledge-hammer effect of the thrice-iterated 'nothing' in the final sentence (remember what a tremendous word that is in the probably-contemporary *Lear*) and the brutality of the last command, 'Uncover, dogs, and lap!' It was Rowe, in Queen Anne's time, who put in the stage-direction about throwing the dishes; there is nothing about it in the Folio, and from the text it seems likelier that Timon is meant to be bombarding his guests with hot water and stones. With a final burst of passionate invective he rushes away, to leave them floundering in undignified confusion among the coats and hats as they try to collect their property and get out of this inhospitable house.

Now comedy is abandoned, for the matter has got beyond a joke. The parallel with *King Lear* is very close, and the parallel with contemporary hazards closer still. Timon's outburst, as he looks back upon the walls of Athens and renounces clothes and civilization together, is reminiscent of Lear stripping off his 'lendings' on the threshold of the hovel, while in the neighbourhood, and perhaps in the very audience, of the Globe there would be many who had known what it was to lose money and friends, be it by simple expenditure and indiscreet hospitality or by the swifter methods of the gaming-table and the cockpit. To them, and to more tranquil playgoers who knew something of their background, the speech must have come as an illustration not of legend but of life.

And so, still more, must have seemed the scene that follows it. Just when Timon has called down fulminations upon the city of Athens and everyone in it, Shakespeare brings in a little gathering of men who have served him and admired him and are themselves ruined and desolate through his ill-fortune. Once again the characteristic epithet is heard,

> Such a house broke,
> So noble a master fallen!

Even as Flavius divides among them the little money he has left, before they take affectionate leave of each other and go this way and that to seek a living as best they may, they find comfort and support in the memory that they share in common, of the noble master they have served. Their hearts, as one of them puts it, still wear Timon's livery (did the hearts of Shakespeare and Heywood still wear Southampton's?), and that thought will do much to sustain them in the life that lies ahead.

But for Timon himself there can be no such consolation. After a shattering disillusionment, and the loss of not only fortune and friends but of ideas that he has taken for granted all his life, his mind has been thrown completely off its balance, and he can never be the same again. The gold that he finds, when root-digging in the wilderness, means nothing to him, nor does Alcibiades' offer of help from his own inadequate store. He is deep in the apathy of melancholia that so often follows a bad nervous breakdown, shrinking instinctively from human contact and from his former pleasure in doing kindnesses with his money. Ill-naturedly he throws gold to Alcibiades for use against Athens, and to that soldier's mistresses, for use against society in general. He reveals it to Apemantus for the sake of scoring off him and disproving the cynic's argument that if he had any money he would hurry back to his old life. When he is visited by three thieves—discontented deserters from Alcibiades' army, if a remark of their commander's is anything to go by—he gives them not only gold but a lecture on the amount of damage that can be done with it, but Shakespeare thinks better of human nature, and makes him defeat his own ends, involuntarily persuading them by his arguments to do the opposite of what he suggests.

There is no obvious call for the continued vehemence and intensity of hate with which these scenes are sometimes played. Swinburne's Ezekiel-Juvenal-Dante figure is inclined to be rather tedious and to make the play drag. Much more interesting, and more pitiable, is the broken solitary who has lost all faith, hope and love for his fellow-men, and has nothing to look forward to but death. Even the visit of Flavius is not really so very welcome; it upsets his latest theory of the general vileness of human nature, and Flavius may be enriched—with the customary injunctions not to do any kindness with it—but must not be allowed to stay and contradict, by his very presence, his old master's bad opinion of mankind.

The discomfiture of the poet and the painter provides a little light relief, but it does not last. Timon is deaf to the apologies and entreaties of the Senators who beg him to return and save Athens from the vengeance of Alcibiades. Power and restitution mean as little to him as does his newly-discovered money, health and living are to him no more than a 'long sickness', and he looks forward only to his end, when Nothing—once again an echo from *King Lear*—will bring him all things. His speech might well, in that age of compulsory church-going, awake recollections of the tremendous close of the Epistle for the first Sunday in Lent—'as deceivers, and yet true; as unknown, and yet well known; as dying, and behold, we live; as chastened, and not killed; as sorrowful, yet alway rejoicing; as poor, yet making many rich; as having nothing, and yet possessing all things'—the ultimate triumph of the Christian ideal.

After that, little remains to be done. His mocking suggestion about the fig-tree was one of the few things about him recorded by Plutarch, so it had to be got in somehow, and though it is not really appropriate to the situation, in it goes. Next moment, after a few lines of moving and impressive sonority, Timon has turned his back on the Senators and the audience, and is gone, never to appear again. The illusions that have been so rudely broken are not to be patched up into a conventional happy ending, and Shakespeare was a realist rather than a romantic. He knew better than to let a reformed Lear win back his throne and his power, despite the fact that the old legend said he did, and Timon in his turn is past recovery. Financial embarrassment may be a matter for amusement in some of its aspects, but it can end in the black tragedy of despair, and none would know this better than the dwellers on Bankside, and the poet who wrote the plays they went to see.

XII

Disguise and Recognition

The Elizabethans—and still more the Jacobeans—liked to see plays about people dressing up and imposing on others who were supposed to be completely taken in by the impersonation. Sometimes their motives were praiseworthy and romantic, at other times—particularly when the author was Ben Jonson—they were reprehensible, extravagant and uproariously funny. The disguise might be necessitated by the course of the plot, as it usually is with Shakespeare, or the plot might be devised deliberately to display the versatility of the leading actor in a variety of quick changes. In 1596, for instance, George Chapman, in *The Blind Beggar of Alexandria*, had written for the Admiral's Men a part in which Alleyn, starting as a shepherd's son, had occasion to disguise himself successively as a duke, a beggar, a money-lender and a fantastically exaggerated character with an eye-patch, a pistol and a theatrically voluminous cloak. More familiar to us are the changes rung by Jonson's characters such as Brainworm in *Every Man in his Humour* and Volpone in the play of that name, not to mention the riot of impersonations carried out by Face, Subtle and Doll Common amid the bustling complications of *The Alchemist*.

Shakespeare's early attempts in this line are crude by comparison with his later achievements. The situation in *The Two Gentlemen of Verona*, where the disguised Julia carries a letter and token to Silvia her unknowing rival, has a charm of its own, but that charm is mitigated for us by our knowledge that he has done the same thing again, and done it a great deal better, in *Twelfth Night*, and the same charge may be levelled at the passage in which her disguise is revealed. It is true that the revelation produces instant repentance and apology in Proteus, but Silvia, whose earlier scene with Julia has prepared us for some expression of pleasure, or at least of interest, on her part, has nothing to say about it at all. Shakespeare, in those days, was a comparative beginner, and the true development of his style was yet to come.

It is possible that someone may have pointed out to him, or it may have been borne in upon him at rehearsal or in performance, that the revelation in this play had its effect on Proteus but hardly attracted the notice, let alone the interest, of the other characters. In *The Comedy of Errors*, at any rate, he works everything up to such an 'intricate impeach' in the last scene that practically everybody is at cross-purposes with everybody else. Though there are no disguises, the play is a maze of mistaken identities involving two pairs of twins, a plaintively possessive wife, a goldsmith clamouring to be paid for goods supplied, a tavern-hostess, an abbess, and an unfortunate old gentleman about to be executed as a prohibited immigrant. In the very first scene we have been told something of the family history, so that we can enjoy the pleasant feeling of knowing more than the various individuals on the stage, but the author has kept a trick up his sleeve by not preparing us for the importance of the abbess. We have known her as a shrewd, humorous and autocratic old lady, neatly puncturing Adriana's indignant self-pity and apparently detached, by her age, her character and her office, from the passions and anxieties of ordinary laymen. It is all the more striking, therefore, when we see her turning from unworldly superiority to very human uncertainty and appeal. The confident authority of her pronouncement at the sight of the bound Aegeon cannot be kept up after its opening lines, and the former mistress of the situation finds herself unexpectedly hesitant to believe in her good fortune. It is all very well to say,

> Whoever bound him, I will loose his bonds
> And gain a husband by his liberty;

but this calm certainty gives way to a very human plea:

> Speak, old Aegeon, if thou be'st the man
> That hadst a wife once called Aemilia

That bore thee at a burden two fair sons:
O, if thou be'st the same Aegeon, speak,
And speak unto the same Aemilia.

and the husband and wife are reunited after nearly a quarter of a century. After that, the reunion with their twin sons and the mutual discovery of the two pairs of brothers are taken practically in a stride, and make less impact, the primary theme being still the resemblance between the twins. The play is, after all, a farce, and a very funny one, so that points like the bewildered Adriana's question to her husband and brother-in-law, 'Which of you two *did* dine with me to-day?' and Dromio's application to the wrong Antipholus about his luggage, are rightly more appropriate to it than serious thankfulness that Aegeon has been redeemed from the executioner's axe.

The disguises of Portia and Rosalind are matters of high comedy as well as being necessitated by the course of the plays in which they appear, and the revelation is with each of them a matter of mirth rather than tense drama, while in *The Merry Wives of Windsor* it is doubtful whether Ford's appearance as Brook can be considered a matter of disguise at all. It has certainly been made so, and recently gave occasion for some diverting business with a false moustache which had a way of falling off and looked very peculiar when hastily replaced upside down, but there is nothing in the text, or the action of the play, that calls for anything of the kind. Falstaff does not know Ford by sight, and most emphatically says so to Ford himself. Ford, when he says 'I have a disguise to sound Falstaff', is using the word in the sense of stratagem or device, and has no need, or intention, to make any change in his appearance. This very fact gives emphasis to Falstaff's discomfiture under Herne's Oak when, ridiculous in his buck's head and assumed horns, he is confronted by Master Brook looking just as usual but with Mrs Ford hanging on his arm and addressing him as 'husband'. The shock here is not the removal of a disguise but the revelation of a familiar figure in an unexpected and unwelcome identity.

As Shakespeare's experience grows, and his style develops, he goes deeper into the minds of his characters, and into the motives for their disguisings, though the shadow of the Swan sometimes falls heavily upon them and hides them from us. How often do we pause to wonder *why* Viola in *Twelfth Night* disguises herself as a boy, or why her brother Sebastian admits to having passed under the name Rodrigo? For us, it is generally enough to assume that people in Shakespeare must be expected to behave like that, or else there would be no play. This is surely doing the poet rather less than justice, and at the same time ignoring indications which might be helpful in our enjoyment of the play.

First of all, we may remember the tradition that the sailors in the second scene bring in a trunk of some sort, indicating that part, at least, of Viola's luggage has been saved from the wreck. Professor Colby Sprague* has gently ridiculed this as unnecessary, but it may be permissible to join issue with him on grounds both of dramatic effect and of practical utility. For one thing, it gives Viola something to sit on, which in this scene makes a lot of difference. For her to play her scene seated, with the captain and sailors standing respectfully before her, establishes her position as a young woman of means, and of some authority. When the captain describes his last sight of Sebastian, and the possibility of his escape, her reply 'For saying so, there's gold' is worthy of Cleopatra, and a little later she casually says 'I'll pay thee bounteously' in a way that shows that though shipwrecked she is by no means destitute. It is the voice of a first-class passenger, possibly even a director of the Line, and the captain obviously obeys it as such.

The sensible course for a well-to-do young woman of good family, suddenly stranded in a foreign country, would be to wait upon the ruler's wife and explain the position. Unfortunately, the prince here is a bachelor, which rules that out, for obvious reasons. The mention of a local Great Lady sounds far more promising, since it should be possible to take an obscure position

* Colby Sprague, A., and Trewin, J. C., *Shakespeare's Plays To-Day*, pp. 28–29. Sidwick & Jackson, London, 1970.

in her household until matters had sorted themselves out, but the captain regretfully explains that the lady is seeing no visitors at present, not even the duke, as she is in deep mourning for her father and brother. Viola's next lines do not really sound like an appeal; they indicate rather that she has considered the captain afresh and decided that he can be trusted, so she goes ahead with yet another plan. The disguise is presented to us not as 'the obvious thing to do, because it is in Shakespeare', but as the best course of the only three that occur to the mind, and there is all the difference in the world. A good deal will have to be done impromptu, as circumstances dictate, but at least a beginning may be made, and her womanly dresses may remain in the captain's charge, as in the last scene she in fact says more than once that they do. We can imagine her rising from her seat and moving on at once, with the little procession after her, to the next stage of her adventure.

In the next act we learn a little more about the family. We have now seen Viola dressed as a boy at Orsino's court, so the entry of a young man looking just like her in attire and (if possible) in features tells us that this must be the missing brother. Antonio has fished him out of the sea and taken a slightly patronizing and protective liking to him, as if doubting whether he is really old enough to go about alone in an unfamiliar country. It comes as a shock to him to know that the supposed Rodrigo is really called Sebastian, and a son of *the* Sebastian of Messaline—obviously a great name in the Mediterranean. His tone changes at once, and becomes less breezy and far more respectful. This young man is a person of position, and it is only natural that he should have decided to remain incognito when first finding himself in strange company. Antonio appreciates that point readily enough, and it tallies with his own conviction that the young man will be the better, after all, for his attendance in the capacity of guide, bodyguard, courier and temporary banker during his stay in Illyria.

With great ingenuity Shakespeare introduces a new variation into his final recognition-scene by making it a matter of hope and expectation to one of the parties but of complete surprise to the other. Antonio's words when he is arrested, and asks the disguised Viola for his money, show her that he takes her for someone whom he has 'snatch'd one half out of the jaws of death'. Next moment he has actually called her by the name of Sebastian, but before she can ask any questions he is hustled away by the duke's officers. But as early as this in the play, it is enough for her. She knows well enough that she looks like her brother, she has imitated his dress when choosing her own, and if there is really someone in the neighbourhood who looks like her, dresses like her, has been rescued by this piratical-looking sea-captain and is actually called Sebastian, it is not too much to hope that her dearly-loved brother may not have perished after all.

Sebastian, meanwhile, is in a very different state of mind. He cannot find his helpful attendant and friend, he is hailed as 'Master Cesario' by a complete stranger, and hit by another one, (who seems absolutely dumbfounded when he hits back with interest), and a truculent and bibulous old gentleman is apparently ready to try more serious conclusions with him. To crown it all, a lady suddenly appears, sends his assailants about their business and invites him into her house in most affectionate terms, and it is not long before she has produced a chaplain and is proposing a secret marriage, to be concealed until he himself shall think fit. It is all most peculiar, he is not sure whether he is mad or dreaming, but he has developed an instant and intense admiration for the lady, and is well content to let matters take their course. Finally, when he comes in to admit apologetically to his bride that he has just broken her kinsman's head in a second brawl, he finds everybody looking at him in amazement, including a splendid-looking personage who is obviously someone in authority, his friend Antonio, apparently under some sort of arrest, and as his gaze travels round, it lights at last upon, apparently, himself. There is a long-standing superstition that to see one's own wraith is a premonition of death, and Shakespeare may well have meant—and told—the player of the part to bear that in mind when challenging this *doppelgänger* with the awed words 'Of charity, what kin are you to me?'

Now that the moment has come, Viola herself is filled with

uncertainty. It is falling out as she has dared to hope, and yet, even at this moment, there may be some trick of fate, making it a spirit, and not the living Sebastian, that stands before her. Sebastian assures her that he is mortal, but cannot yet be quite certain who this is, who claims to be a child of Sebastian of Messaline. If it were a woman, he would know what name to give her, and here he gives a proof that to her is all-convincing, and that to us has been obscured and almost nullified by our familiarity with the play. He speaks her name.

We know *Twelfth Night* so well, from reading it, seeing it, or studying it at school or university for the purpose of being examined upon it, that we think of its charming heroine as Viola from the first moment of her appearance on the stage. But, let us remember, the play's first audience would not, and could not, do anything of the sort. They could not have read the play, as it was not in print until 1623, and the only name by which the heroine had gone, up to this point, was the assumed one of Cesario. When Sebastian says 'Viola', he speaks a name that conveys nothing to anyone in the company except its owner, and even now she hesitates to identify herself without a little supporting evidence. The mole on her father's brow, the fact of his death on her 13th birthday, are tentatively named and eagerly accepted, and it is safe for her to admit, without fear of rejection, the secret of her 'masculine usurp'd attire'. This in its turn leads the duke to realize that he too can be the gainer by the revelation. He looks forward to seeing Viola in her own clothes, we are reminded once again that they are in safe keeping with the Captain (doubtless in that traditional trunk), and the news of the latter's temporary imprisonment leads us back to Malvolio and the merry conclusion of the play.

The duke's disguise in *Measure for Measure* is plausible enough visually, as the cowled head and downcast eyes of the seeming friar are very different from the imperious bearing of the ruler of Vienna. Vocally, on the other hand, the part must have called for some degree of co-operation on the part of the audience, notably in the last scene of Act III, where he has a short conversation with Escalus, the old councillor who might very well be expected to recognize him. It is significant that in this little scene the duke speaks almost entirely in prose, avoiding the stately and impressive periods in which he talks to those who are not so familiar with him in his true colours, and these may well be many. To Angelo in the first scene and to Friar Thomas in the third he has said that he has never liked to 'stage himself' to the eyes of his subjects, or to 'haunt assemblies', but has 'ever loved the life removed'. More than one commentator has seen in these lines a complimentary allusion to the retiring habits of king James. Something of that, indeed, there may be, but if so it is surely no more than a secondary consideration. The main function of this insistence is to indicate that the duke's subjects have no reason to know him well by sight. Once that is understood, his miscellaneous wanderings and conversations in disguise are far easier to accept, and particularly easy for an audience in the first months of a new reign, when the general public did not yet know what their own king really looked like. He had taken his time to come down from Scotland, when he got to the outskirts of London he 'rode in a coach somewhat closely from the Charterhouse to Whitehall, and from thence he was conveyed by water to the Tower of London', so that the populace as a whole saw very little of him. Stow, who gives this account, was probably one of the disappointed ones. It was all very different from the public processions of Elizabeth, and it made it all the easier to believe, in an age without Press photography and the present swift transmission of visual images, how even the greatest of public figures might go about in disguise without much fear of detection.

His disclosure in the last scene is sudden and dramatic, with a jack-in-the-box effect that Shakespeare does not use elsewhere. Zurbaran's painting of a Franciscan, in the National Gallery, shows how good a mask the cowl of a religious order can be, but though it can be pulled back effectively in the moment of climax, the cassock and corded girdle cannot be so easily cast aside. They must stay on, and the actor (Burbage, probably, when the play was put on before king James on Boxing Night in 1604) has to be sufficiently ducal and imposing about the head and stance to distract attention from the deliberate poverty of his body-garments. This is not always easy, and quite possibly Shakespeare found out as much when it came to performance. Certainly, as will be seen, he was less abrupt when handling a somewhat similar episode in a later play.

In *King Lear*, both Kent and Edgar have to spend a good deal of their time in disguise. Kent, having been banished for insubordination unbecoming in a councillor, enjoys much more freedom of speech as a blunt and cynical serving-man. His claim to appreciate the authority in Lear's bearing is an ironic sequel to the fact that it was his own disregard of that same authority, when he disagreed with it, that got him dismissed from court and banished from the country, but it is also the least likely attitude to remind the king of his rash and disrespectful councillor. Once accepted, he is able to continue in the character he has chosen, of a sturdy, independent servant, loyal but sharply critical, abrupt to his master and overbearing to almost everybody else, like a combination of Humphrey Wasp in *Bartholomew Fair* and Queen Victoria's dogged and unpopular John Brown. Edgar, on the other hand, has to show much more versatility. First he plays poor Tom the madman, mopping and mowing in a blanket; then, when he has got some clothes on, his speech becomes so much more reasonable that his blind father notices the difference and comments on it, and later in the same scene, after the cliff incident, he represents himself as a casual passer-by. The player of Edgar has a chance of showing his talent for variety of impersonation.

Towards the close of his career, Shakespeare seems to have been more and more deeply concerned with the thought of reunion with persons long lost and mourned for. In almost all his last plays this theme recurs, sometimes involving disguises, sometimes not. There is no disguising in *Pericles*, *Prince of Tyre*, but that uneven play contains two of the loveliest recognition-scenes the poet ever wrote. King Pericles, mourning for his wife and daughter, is a man without hope. He has seen his beloved wife coffined and cast into the sea; years later he has been shown his daughter's tomb in Tarsus, and he is now unshaven, clad in sackcloth and sunk in the apathy of despair. His gradual awakening to perception of those around him, then to speech and at last to amazed recognition of his daughter is portrayed with an extraordinary wealth and variety of natural emotion. First he merely grunts when Marina speaks to him, then, in a few disjointed words, he seems to have got some notion of what she is talking about. At this point, it is clear, he turns and looks at her, and is so far roused from his melancholy as to find relief in tears at her resemblance to his wife. His emotions are waking again, to the extent that he is interested in her and asks to hear her story, but as she tells it he is more and more fiercely disturbed. Her name Marina, and the statements that she was born at sea and that her mother was a king's daughter, rouse him to such a pitch of excitement that she is alarmed and tries to stop, but he questions her still further, and she tells of her escape from murder, and her capture by the pirates who brought her to Mitylene. By this time her lines show that his behaviour is terrifying her, and that he himself is passionately clasping her and scrutinizing her through his tears, so in self-defence she cries out the one thing that she has never disclosed to anyone in the city—her father's name:

> But, good sir,
> Whither will you have me? Why do you weep? It may be
> You think me an impostor; no, good faith;
> I am the daughter to King Pericles
> If good King Pericles be!

The scene between the two is almost operatic in its intensity. For the first time for months Pericles becomes conscious of those about him. He calls Helicanus by name, telling him the good news, then turns back to Marina, who is increasingly bewildered at his transports, and asks her mother's name, to which she replies by asking him his own. The answer comes like a hammer-stroke, and crowns the whole:

> I am Pericles of Tyre: but tell me now
> My drown'd queen's name, as in the rest you said

> Thou hadst been godlike perfect,
> The heir of kingdoms, and another like
> To Pericles thy father.

Each has been revealed to each. The succeeding lines show us that by this time Marina is on her knees at her father's feet, giving the confirmation that both know to be superfluous now,

> Is it no more to be your daughter than
> To say my mother's name was Thaisa?
> Thaisa was my mother, who did end
> The minute I began.

Next moment he is blessing her, raising her and calling for fresh garments to replace his penitential sackcloth, trying to tell Helicanus what has happened, asking who Lysimachus is and what he is doing there, and finally, incoherent with joy, collapsing on to his bed and falling into an exhausted sleep.

After all this, it would seem impossible to include another recognition-scene without anticlimax, but Shakespeare succeeds in doing it, none the less. This time there is no obvious problem to be resolved at the opening; Pericles is a normal man again, coming in state to do sacrifice to Diana at Ephesus, as commanded in a dream. He is not expecting any further revelations; when one of the priestesses interrupts his thanksgiving by crying out his name and falling in a faint, he is naturally surprised and concerned, but no more, and when old Cerimon tells him that this must be his long-lost wife, he is polite but incredulous. The emotional speech this time comes from Thaisa, torn between consciousness of her sacred office and recognition of a 'voice and favour' that have been lost to her for years. It is more like the appeal of the Abbess in that earlier play about Ephesus, but handled with a more finely finished artistry:

> O let me look!
> If he be none of mine, my sanctity
> Will to my sense lend no licentious ear,
> But curb it, spite of seeing. O my lord,
> Are you not Pericles? Like him you speak,

> Like him you are: did you not name a tempest,
> A birth, and death?

Pericles recognizes the voice, but not, it seems, the face. Possibly, since Thaisa is serving as a priestess, the author intended her to be veiled; at any rate the features that Pericles claimed to see repeated in her daughter arouse no comment when he sees them face to face. He himself is altered by a 14-year-old beard, but when he cries 'Immortal Dian!' he must be meant to throw up his hands in a gesture of wonder or adoration, for Thaisa sees his ring, and reminds him how her father gave him one like it at Pentapolis. This little detail carries complete conviction, and he bursts out impulsively:

> This, this; no more, you gods! your present kindness
> Makes my past miseries sport: you shall do well
> That on the touching of her lips I may
> Melt, and no more be seen.

and in a moment she is in his arms. The play ends in a matter of minutes, before we can recover from the sense of what John Masefield once called 'that strange, touching, very Shakespearean romance, of the thing long lost beautifully recovered before the end, so that the last years of the chief man in the play may be happy and complete.'

The play about which Masefield wrote those words was not *Pericles* but *Cymbeline*, which has in the course of its action three disguises and a collection of assorted revelations in the last scene of all, so many and so complicated that the scene has more than once become a target for gentle and not-so-gentle ridicule from the literary-minded. But we must remember that it was not written to be read. It was written for the stage, and on the stage the variety of voices, characters and emotions takes away the main feeling of repetitiveness, and keeps the spectator 'in full drama' throughout.

It is not amiss, also, to remember the story of a 17th-century duke of Brandenburg who was on the point of offering battle when one of his officers pointed out in alarm that the enemy's forces outnumbered his own by 10,000 men, to which the duke replied at once, 'Go on, go on! You must always leave *something* for God Almighty to do!' and won his battle. Shakespeare in this scene has left something in the way of emotional acting for Cymbeline to do; after having had a pretty dull time through four acts of the play the king is allowed a chance to give a virtuoso performance in the fifth. Not all Cymbelines have had the capacity to take it.

Of the disguises, Imogen's passing for a boy is acceptable partly because it is a personal necessity for Imogen and only secondarily a dramatic necessity for Shakespeare. Her belief in Postumus' death, because she sees Cloten's headless body wearing her husband's clothes, ought not to strike us as far-fetched after the number of detective stories in which an unrecognizable corpse has been wrongly identified on just such evidence.

Postumus himself has to turn his coat twice in the last act. At the beginning of it he comes in wearing what he calls 'Italian weeds', but announces that though he has come to Britain with the invading Roman army, he will not fight against Imogen's native land, but hopes to earn his death in its defence. His concluding couplet,

> To shame the guise o' the world, I will begin
> The fashion, less without and more within,

suggests that he takes off his outer garments, presumably a cloak, breastplate and hat or burgonet, leaves them in a corner of the stage and goes out in his shirt-sleeves. The march-past of the two armies gives him time to put on something suitable to Jacobean ideas of an Ancient Briton—possibly a ragged cloak of the shaggy type still worn at the time by Irish irregulars—and go past, as the stage direction has it, 'like a poor soldier'. So attired, he disarms Iachimo, helps in the rescue of Cymbeline, and later describes the battle to a runaway British lord; but a dozen lines after the latter's departure he declares that he has 'resum'd again the part he came in', and in another minute or two he is arrested and taken prisoner as a Roman by a patrol who are actually looking for the 'fourth man in a silly habit' who had done so well in the field. Once more the unlocalized Elizabethan stage must have been helpful. The 'Italian weeds' have been lying undisturbed where he left them, and he has only to pick them up and put them on, or even sling them loosely about him, to be imprisoned and condemned as he desires.

The last scene, with all its revelations, is designed to be dominated by Cymbeline. At the outset he is shown contented and triumphant, owning his indebtedness to the two young warriors from the hills and their elderly guardian, knighting them all three and lamenting the absence of their mysterious helper. Hard upon that, he receives his first shock in the news of his queen's death and her deathbed declaration of hate for him and for her stepdaughter Imogen, and it is in this mood of disillusion that he receives his Roman captives—including Iachimo, Postumus and the disguised Imogen herself—and coldly bids them prepare for death. When Caius Lucius pleads for the life of the supposed Fidele, who 'hath done no Briton harm, though he have served a Roman', he sees something familiar in the young page's face, and takes him to his favour, taking care to explain that this is done for his own sake, and owes nothing to his master's pleading.

That starts off the whole chain-reaction of recognitions. Iachimo is made to explain his possession of Postumus' ring, and when he tells how he won it by an unworthy stratagem, Cymbeline's eager listening is interrupted by the outburst and indignant confession of Postumus, who blames himself miserably for Imogen's death, only to discover a few lines later that she is alive and at his feet. Both her husband and her father have misjudged her deeply, and are deeply repentant. Explanations from Cornelius and Pisanio make matters clearer still, until Cymbeline is brought up short, when hearing of Cloten's journey to Wales, by Guiderius' interjection

Let me end the story
I slew him there.

Regretfully enough, Cymbeline feels bound to invoke the law, and send Guiderius to execution, when old Belarius checks him

IV Irish soldiers, sketched from life. The shaggy, tattered mantle of the central figure suggests the type of garment that could be assumed by Postumus in *Cymbeline* when disguising himself as a 'poor soldier' in the army of the Britons.

with the surprising claim that 'This man is better than the man he slew.' The king's rage is rising like Lear's at the suggestion of opposition, still more at the discovery that the old warrior is that Belarius whom he banished 20 years ago, and he is ordering his arrest in turn when he is confronted, at the height of his anger, with the astounding challenge that the young man whom he is condemning to death is in fact his own son, and therefore senior to the queen's son Cloten. The news is so unexpected, and so welcome, that he can hardly speak, but stands silent and intent while Belarius tells the story of his flight with the children and their nurse, and his training of them to grow up in ignorance of their parentage. It all seems too good to be true. Belarius s speaking of evidence, of 'a most curious mantle' in which Arviragus was wrapped, and which he can easily produce, but Cymbeline knows that he must not let himself believe too readily in his good fortune. The child Guiderius had, he remembers, a mole upon his neck, which would not be easy to counterfeit. It is too much to hope for, that this should be really he, birthmark and all, but next moment Belarius is assuring him that this is so. The natural reaction to his impetuous fury is to find himself exhausted and on the verge of tears, but, in his own words, 'a mother to the birth of three'. Imogen, who for a few minutes had been to all appearances her father's heiress, is told that she has 'lost by this a kingdom', but with a true Shakespearean antithesis she answers him with a triple contradiction,

No, my lord,
I have *got—two—worlds* by it.

She is happy enough in the realization that the young hunters who called her their brother in the wilderness are her brothers in very deed.

After this, the revelation of Postumus as 'the forlorn soldier that so nobly fought' is hesitantly admitted by himself and confirmed by the repentant Iachimo, who kneels and submits himself to his former victim's mercy. Here, again, the critics are perhaps over-ready to accuse Postumus, as they have accused Hal and Edgar in the past, of being priggish and sententious when he is really being sincere. Iachimo may have basely slandered Imogen, but Postumus feels that he has been as base, or more so, to have believed Iachimo. He cannot, and will not, set himself up in judgement over the other; the most he can say, in the way even of criticism, is his exhortation to 'live, and deal with others better'. Cymbeline takes his cue from his son-in-law—the first time he has acknowledged him as such—and the play ends upon a note of general pardon and peace. So long a series of successive revelations and recognitions is apt to look incredible, and slightly ridiculous, on the printed page, but once again it was not written to be read, but heard in the theatre, and illuminated by the reactions of the various characters involved, and most of all by the passionate and changing moods of Cymbeline. Unlike Pericles or Aegeon, he himself has been largely responsible for his own bereavement, and he and Postumus alike can say no more than 'pardon's the word for all', because they have learned how great has been their own need for pardon.

This sentiment lies behind what is probably the best-known recognition scene in all Shakespeare—the statue scene in *The Winter's Tale.* This is at once the climax of the last act and the direct, unquestioned consequence of the first. At the very opening of the play, Leontes is needlessly suspicious of his queen, and in succession he is seen accusing her, misjudging her, losing her and bitterly repenting his injustice. At long last, when Perdita—'that which was lost', as the oracle called her—has been found and restored to him, his penance and purgation are accomplished, he is let into Paulina's secret, and discovers again his lost, much-wronged and all-forgiving Hermoine. The theme is so important to the continuity of the play that the secondary recognition-scenes are not allowed to distract attention from it. They take place off-stage, and we hear of them only in the conversation of others. The Bohemian scenes, the courtship of Florizel and the manifold disguises of Autolycus—who carries through his impersonations with the enthusiasm of Jonson's Brainworm—form a delightful interlude between the tragic tension of the third act and the serene beauty of the fifth, but they have nothing to do with the courting, parting and reconcilement of Leontes and Hermione, and Polixenes and Florizel must attend in the last scene as beholders, not participants in that act of reunion. The loyal, fearless and uncompromising Paulina has a place in it, and deserves one. She, and she only, has known that Hermione was still living. For a change, Shakespeare did not even let the audience know of it, though from our reading of the play, and reading about it even if we have not seen it, we take for granted that everybody knows it now.

There is a revelation, and something in the way of a disguise, in the last scene of *The Tempest*, where Prospero is specifically mentioned in the stage direction as entering 'in his magic robes'. As in *Measure for Measure*, a disguised duke has to reveal himself and dominate the scene, but this time the author has made the disguise rather easier to get out of. A friar's frock does not open down the front, and cannot be shed in a hurry, and it is difficult to wear a hat, coronet, or headdress of any impressiveness under a friar's cowl, especially when that cowl has to be pulled off with deliberate incivility by a fellow-actor. A magician's robes, however, would be the all-enveloping equivalent of the scientist's laboratory overall, and can be designed to suit the requirements of the management, the player and the play. What is important, in this scene, is the splendour they reveal. Prospero's use of the word 'discase' shows that he is casting something off, rather than putting anything on. The magic garment is discarded like Bedford's mourning-cloak at the funeral of Henry V, and the duke of Milan stands there arrayed as the prince he is. There has been no scuffling; Ariel has a song with which to cover such time as it takes to undo the necessary fastenings, and stands by, like a footboy, with the only things that could not be worn under the robes and have had to be specially asked for—the hat and rapier. He duly clips the sword on to its belt-hook and hands his master the hat—probably not a crown, but the plumed hat of a gentleman of fashion. It is the triumph of the exile's return to civilization, that he should be in a position to say, in effect, 'Boy, bring me my hat and stick,' and be ready for the world again.

But there is one more recognition yet to come, and one that

can be made infinitely more moving, in performance, than a casual reading would suggest. Alonzo of Naples has spent most of the play in grief for the supposed death of his son, while that same son, Ferdinand, laments that his father's death in the storm has made him king of Naples. When Prospero leads Alonzo and his companions to his cell on the island, and shows Ferdinand and Miranda happily playing chess, the mutual recognition is brilliantly differentiated. Alonzo, like others before him, hardly dares to believe that things can really be as they seem. There is something of Pericles' fear to accept the tempting fact, when he says at last:

> If this prove
> A vision of the island, one dear son
> Shall I twice lose.

Ferdinand, on the contrary, has no doubt whatever. He accepts the miracle unquestioning, and there is a ring of both awe and gladness in his very simple words,

> Though the seas threaten, they are merciful,
> I have cursed them without cause.

Next moment he is on his knees, to receive his father's blessing as a good son should, and Shakespeare's last known recognition-scene is over.

Epilogue

Once one has got on to these terms with Shakespeare, it is incredible how many occasions there are on which he keeps cropping up in unexpected contexts. In my own experience, sentry duty in the small hours of the morning brought home the fact that what a sentry really thinks about is the punctuality—or otherwise—of his relief, and sure enough, the minds of the sentries in *Hamlet* and *Antony and Cleopatra* turn in exactly the same direction. Turn over the pages of the first edition of Holinshed, and a picture of Macbeth and Banquo catches the eye, in their confrontation with the Weird Sisters. For all we know, it may have caught Shakespeare's eye in the same way, and led him on to read the chronicler's account of the episode and what came of it. Browse in the book, as one is tempted to do, and up comes a chapter headed 'Of English Dogges', and consisting of a dissertation epitomized in Macbeth's reflections on the subject when engaging a couple of bad characters to commit a murder for him. Delve a little into the history and topography of Elizabethan London, and several of Hotspur's jokes to his wife take on a special significance for the local audience that first saw *King Henry IV* in the Theatre (first of that name) in Finsbury Fields. Look at the early picture-maps of London and the Thames, and the tiny representation of the Royal Barge, with its team of watermen and the upstanding weapons of its armed escort, may recall Enobarbus' description of that other barge, that 'like a burnished throne burned on the water' as it bore Cleopatra to her first sight of Antony.

With correspondence and contemporary chronicles it is just the same. King James's Ambassador to the Mogul emperor Jahangir describes the audience-hall in detail, specifically comparing it architecturally to a theatre, and adds a remark or two showing that in the theatres of his day a player king 'in his state' was enthroned as a matter of course upon the upper stage. John Stow, or rather his editor and elaborator Edmund Howes, describes one or two episodes of animal-baiting in the Tower, and mentions incidentally that in 1609 the Tower lions were pitted against 'a greate and fierce Beare' that had lately killed a child, but that the lions were none of them keen to attack it, taking refuge in their dens at the first opportunity. Shortly after that episode appeared *The Winter's Tale*, in which Antigonus is pursued and killed off-stage by a hunted bear. Commentators have been patronizingly witty about that bear, but the chronicler's reference throws a good deal more light upon the matter. Shakespeare's theatre-public of that period was very much a bear-garden public as well, and knew better than to think of bears as benevolent and slightly comic. A good many spectators of *The Winter's Tale* might well have seen that 'killer bear' baited to death upon a scaffold by the king's command. (We are told, at least, that the dead child's mother was given £20 out of the gate-money, which implies that the baiting must have been very fully attended.) The playwright knew that a bear was a wild beast, and that a baited or hunted bear was a savage, dangerous and terrible one, and he could be sure that his audience knew it too.

It would be easy to multiply such instances, but there is no need. The interested reader will find them for himself, and will gain all the more pleasure from the finding. These chapters may have helped to start him on his way, but that is all. They make no pretence of covering all the problems and possibilities, nor, for that matter, all the plays. They are no more than personal conclusions drawn by one Shakespearean playgoer from a study of the plays and, to some extent, of the London in which they first appeared. Yet, perhaps, they may point the way for others to read Shakespeare with greater pleasure and understanding, to their own advantage and to that of those whom they may call in their turn to share their enjoyment. One can but echo the closing words of those editors who began it all by first printing the plays in folio: 'And such readers we wish him'.

Index

Index